The Wings of the Wind

SANG HEE KWAK

ISBN 978-1-965679-11-1 (Paperback)
ISBN 978-1-965679-18-0 (Hardback)
ISBN 978-1-965679-12-8 (Ebook)

Inquiries and Book Orders should be addressed to:

Leavitt Peak Press
17901 Pioneer Blvd Ste L #298, Artesia, California 90701
Phone #: 2092191548

Prologue

Arirang Peace Farm

Ah, four and a half centuries have passed; how distant it feels!

December, which was frozen stiff, has passed, and January, February, March, and April have also gone by, and May has arrived - the butterfly's apparition on top of Park Jae-hoon's grave dances in front of Ji-ae. When the wind blows, the butterflies gather.

A swarm of butterflies dances around an outdoor stage. The butterflies dance around the square, fluttering between branches of various flowers, such as mugunghwa, azalea, and jinddalae, sent from all over the world.

The sparrows fly around, fluttering from branch to branch, shaking them as they go. The trees are small evergreens, acacias, and many other unknown and strange trees standing in rows.

Moving away from the Arirang Peace Farm, a grand opening ceremony for the World Youth Arirang Center is being held with a concert on the makeshift outdoor stage filled to the brim with a North-South joint choir of 400 members and an orchestra of over 100 members as if it were about to burst at the seams.

The front row is filled with children from around the world, representatives from various countries, and representatives of North and South Korean civilians. Behind them, the general audience fills the seats.

No sound can be heard. Astonishingly, all sounds are silenced with mouths shut tight. Following this, the boisterous orchestra strikes up, drumming out a beat that resonates throughout the venue. The waterfalls of Mount Geumgang burst, and the tumultuous waters of the Daedong River, the Amnok River, and the Dumangang River, as well as the Han River, the Seomjin River, and the Nakdong River, all flow together to embrace the whole land of Korea. The waves overflow, enveloping Dokdo Island and Namdo Island, while iridescent flags flutter in the air. As the orchestral performance softens, a poignant and joyous duet in both male and female voices flows.

Just as winter gives way to spring,
Oh, how the years have slipped away.
Oh, the vines of arrowroots, tough and stubborn love,
That single drop of blood
Flows and flows throughout
The mountains and rivers of Korea
While the East Sea pounds against the sky.
And the roses and jinddalae flowers bloom bright red.
Incessant step of our people from Baekdudaegan Mountain Range,
The face of the wind.

"The moon surfaced in her thoughts. Why, at such a moment, did he come to mind? He is the dragon slumbering in the depths of her being. Ah, is he yet another trap for me? Or is he my wings?

The sound of patients' slippers dragging along the corridor intermittently reaches her ears, mingled only with the footsteps of visitors. The hospital is as silent as the bottom of the sea.

"I can't bear it any longer. I might go back to Korea... I feel like I'm going insane."

When an invitation came from a university in Korea, his sigh, heavier than the guilt of leaving his family behind, carried these words.

"Just go. It will probably be for the best. You don't have to worry about us."

At that moment, Jiae chose to let him go rather than cling to his presence. Has he now cured the illness he spoke of? Quenched that burning thirst?

The airport, as always, was congested with traffic and teeming with people. She barely managed to park the car in front of the building adorned with the Korean Air sign. Crossing the pedestrian lane, she walked towards the waiting area. The airport lounge was, as ever, bustling with people, a quiet simmer of anticipation filling the air.

"The Korean Air flight scheduled to arrive at nine tonight will be delayed due to weather conditions in Anchorage and is expected at ten."

The crisp voice of a female announcer flowed from the loudspeaker.

"Damn it! When has it ever been on time..."

A middle-aged man standing next to Jiae grumbled. The plane arrived 30 minutes later than the announcer had foretold. She calmly greeted him, the man who emerged ahead of other travelers, carrying only a handbag.

"How was your flight?"

As they exited the winding airport driveway, the car began to pick up speed. It was then that Jiae spoke. He gave no response, merely glancing at her briefly before returning his gaze to the night view of the airport. A surge of emotions, a mix of sadness and thirst, sharply pricked her throat. Who said sadness was sweet? My sadness, what is it? A poisonous mushroom? Am I a tick, lying in a swamp of deep, impenetrable despair, waiting to emerge? Is he the iron fetter, the chain that keeps me from flying far? Is all this his fault?

"Is Jaesik doing well?"

He spoke after a while, still looking ahead.

"Yes, he called a few days ago. Seems he's dating an American. But he said she's more Korean than Koreans. Apparently, she's a child of American parents who grew up in Korea.""

""Hmm!"

As evening approached, a drizzle turned into heavier rain, obscuring the view. Jiae slowed down her car as the rain intensified. Other vehicles sped by in the rain. Briefly, a woman's face flitted through her mind, a woman she didn't know personally, just heard of as someone from her hometown. What had become of that woman and her relationship? Why did he choose an old flame from his hometown, of all people? But what does it matter to me? Right then, a loud clang of metal cut through the sky. Jiae's hand trembled like a sparrow's wing caught in the wind.

Yes, it was raining. 20 years ago, on the day she left her homeland, it had rained too. As the rain eased and she settled into her Northwest Airlines seat, uncontrollable tears welled up. For some reason, she felt like she'd never see her mother again. The reason wasn't clear.

She lifted the white window cover and looked out. The people standing in clusters resembled islands floating in the middle of the ocean, giving a sense of unreality. Is that my homeland? The homeland seen from a plane, setting off into the distance. The word 'homeland,' formless and indistinct. Her mother leaned her head on her uncle's shoulder.

"Don't act recklessly just because it's a foreign country, where nobody knows you. When you're abroad, you represent South Korea. Do you understand, Jiae? You're a civilian ambassador of South Korea. People will see South Korea through you. You must always conduct yourself properly, Jiae."

How many times had her mother repeated those words last night? Listening to her mother, Jiae wondered what joy her mother had found in life. Touching her mother's wrinkled face, her heart ached. Her mother's words on the last night before her daughter's departure etched deeply in her heart.

Now, the rain had completely stopped. Against the backdrop of the hazy transmission tower and the people, Hyun's face came to mind. From deep within her heart, a thorny bundle stirred and spread throughout her body.

"Young lady, is this your first time?"

The elderly gentleman already seated next to Jiae spoke in Korean with an American accent.

"You'll get used to it after one or two trips. It's like that for everyone at first. But remember, young lady, our homeland, our hometown, is always in our hearts.

Whether we realize it or not, it remains deeply rooted in our hearts over time, part of our blood and flesh. Just as humans can't live without air, as fish can't survive out of water, no matter how much time passes, some things remain unchanged. That's our hometown, our homeland, young lady.""

"The elderly gentleman murmured to himself, his voice gaining strength, almost as if he was making a vow with his last words. Was he a laborer in the sorghum fields in his youth, now finally returning to his homeland to soothe his nostalgia? Who was this old man? What circumstances had forced him to leave his beloved country?

A story of a lonely old man she had read in the social section of the newspaper surfaced in her thoughts. He had lived his entire life in America and, upon reaching his seventies, returned home, not revealing his identity, living under the care of a kind soul. In the end, he passed away quietly, leaving all his wealth to his caregiver.

"Student, during the era of Japanese imperialism, we had to abandon our farmlands, turn our backs on our beloved hometowns, and head to Manchuria, Sakhalin, or even Japan. It was a forced migration. Many who were taken away for forced labor have yet to return. Student, history doesn't lie. Whatever is sown must be reaped. You must understand how terrifying the honesty of history can be. Now, students like you leave their motherland, nurtured by it, to chase bigger dreams."

The plane started to move. The old man, seemingly exhausted, closed his eyes. His face, still showing signs of vitality, was ruddy, with deep wrinkles etched into his cheeks like cracks on a parched field. They spread from his jawline, encircling his neck like a collar.

Jiae thought of her mother, who had lived her life solely for her daughter. The only time she felt her father's affection was during the last few years they lived in Japan.

After liberation, her father brought them back to their hometown, staying like a traveler for a night before leaving again.

After her grandfather passed away and Jiae graduated from elementary school, her mother sold the remaining land and moved to Seoul, where her family was from.

Her father began to stay at home when Jiae was in the first year of high school. Since then, the smell of medicinal herbs being boiled for him never ceased in their home. One day, overhearing a conversation between her parents, Jiae trembled with profound betrayal upon learning about her father's secret life, including a child with another woman. Was this the result of his so-called patriotic activities, roam-

5

ing around China and abroad? What then became of that woman? By a twist of fate, after the child's death and the woman's demise due to chronic illness, her father returned to his legal wife. Her mother silently accepted him back and cared for him devotedly. It wasn't even two years before her father passed away from stomach cancer."

"Subtitle: Wounds

Jiae immersed herself in her studies, seemingly forgetting about the vacation, diligently focusing on her lagging department. She paid no mind to fellow students who either returned to their hometowns or sought summer jobs. She cherished the solitude of the empty campus, burying herself in her studies to forget the summer heat.

As the long summer day waned and the sun dipped below the western forest, evening approached. The sound of someone approaching and the voice of the landlady were heard outside.

"Jiae, someone's here to see you. Says they're a friend."

"Ah, must be someone from Korea!"

With a sigh of relief, he wiped the sweat from his forehead.

"I made a point to come this way."

As the stranger approached Jiae, his face reddened. Jiae had guessed he was a Korean student from the moment she saw him walking along the narrow path between the tall trees. Students of different ethnicities passed by them, indifferent to their conversation.

"By the way, my name is Park Jaehoon."

He extended his hand.

"I'm Lee Jiae."

That day, Jiae had an early dinner and was wrestling with her textbooks, preparing for exams. She was also anxious about an assignment due the following week. Determined to return home the next year, she put aside the book she had been curiously examining last summer and opened the door.

"I'm sorry for showing up like this."

"I have something important I need to tell Jiae."

The sudden visit made Jiae's face contort in surprise.

"I thought this person was a friend of Jiae, I'm sorry."

The landlady, not understanding Korean, looked back and forth between the two, apologizing.

"It's okay."

Jiae reassured the embarrassed old lady with a smile.

"I'm sorry."

He looked at her for a moment, shy like a young boy, then sat on the sofa that Jiae used as a bed at night.

"It's a nice place. Close to the school, cozy... You seem to be quite talented, Jiae.""

""Not at all. It's not my talent, but a missionary I met in Korea became friends with a professor here."

Jiae sat down on the chair at the table she used as both a desk and dining table.

"Oh, is that so? Are you a Christian, Jiae?"

"Well, just... I don't know."

Jiae's gaze was fixed on the wall, where a shadow faintly flickered. The lid of the kettle clattered, urging her to fill the empty cups.

"I don't take sugar."

He declined with a wave of his hand. Jiae carried the cups over and sat down. He sipped his coffee silently. The silence was uncomfortable for Jiae. Why had he come, uninvited? What could be so important that he had to say? The darkening room began to weigh on her. She got up, turned on the light, and sat back down to finish her tea.

"Um... Jiae?"

"...?"

"I said earlier that I have something to tell you."

Jiae wordlessly sent a glance towards his neat, white forehead. In the light, she noticed beads of sweat.

"Jiae, will you marry me?"

Jiae couldn't believe her ears. Her eyes widened in shock.

"What are you saying?"

"I'm asking you to marry me."

He leaned back slightly, his disheveled expression superimposed on her startled face. Her lips parted slightly as she stared at him. Had she heard him right? Proposing marriage? To her, after barely two years of acquaintance?

A strained smile appeared on his face, his eyes awkwardly meeting hers.

"Jiae, about my proposal..."

"No, how can you...!"

His gaze was insistent.

"I'm serious, Jiae."

"Marry... you?"

Jiae wanted to take it as a joke. She felt overwhelmed by his intense gaze.

"How can you say such a thing, even as a joke?"

An exaggerated tone escaped Jiae's mouth, and she swiftly turned her head away."

""It's not a joke. I've given it a lot of thought," he asserted, straightening his shoulders and steadying his voice.

"Of course, if it's inconvenient for you right now, I'm willing to wait. Why should fellow students, lonely from studying abroad, live like this? Wouldn't it be better to support each other, to live together...?"

"Stop! Please, just stop!"

Jiae, almost without realizing, waved her hands dismissively, her voice rising. She wanted to accuse him of cowardice, but the words choked her.

"We could be happy," he insisted.

After saying this with a lingering note of regret, he quickly finished the rest of his coffee, then turned his head towards the door. Jiae didn't notice the fleeting shadow of loneliness and stubborn, rusted anger on his face turned away. She only felt the disarray akin to that of a patient sitting before a doctor for treatment. As if reaching out, pleading, her voice softened.

"I've never even considered something like marriage, no matter how hard or lonely it gets."

"Jiae, I came to South Korea alone during the Korean War. At the age of fifteen, with my father gone, my mother, in tears because of my younger siblings, pushed me alone towards the south. I don't even know if they're alive or dead."

Was this supposed to be related to his proposal? No more words came from Jiae's lips. She sat as if breathless, her gaze pinned to the wall, while time painfully twisted and flowed away.

He awkwardly got up, bowed his head towards Jiae, and then walked away through the dimming streets, passing through the door she silently opened for him. Jiae felt a burden watching his retreating figure. And then, something like a festering wound refusing to heal, stirred within her. As if soothing a whining child to sleep.

A throbbing pain, speaking of the world's vague and undefined loneliness and suffering – where had it been sleeping all this time? Lying silently under someone else's floor, rising occasionally without any reason or excuse – what are you? The smoke of despair and anxiety emanating from your breath.

I can't endure you. Stay still, I won't touch you either, I'll just pass by you. Was that the light that Hyun talked about? It didn't seem so. It seemed like a forbidden topic that should be left alone. Mr. Park's mention of happiness briefly crossed her mind. But does the bluebird of happiness even exist? For him to boldly claim we could be happy... Yes, the subject of Hyun's sentences was always one. Human was human, person was person."

"Jiae no longer wanted to dwell on these thoughts. Feeling ignorant and useless in the face of such logic, like a worn-out pencil, she shook her head. Park Jaehoon's courtship was persistent. In the library, on the campus grounds, his eyes and gestures beseeched her.

"Marry me. Please, marry me." Even when he wasn't there, his presence clung to her like a tick. Jiae gritted her teeth and focused on her studies, eager to graduate and return to Korea where her mother and Hyun awaited.

That day, as she was leaving the library, she unexpectedly bumped into Park Jaehoon in the campus grounds. It was twilight. Walking together through the lush southern campus, he shared his story.

"Being pushed by my mother's hand to safety was purely a stroke of luck. Amidst other refugees, I crossed countless life-threatening hurdles, passing by the Han River. Arriving in Busan, where could a boy with no kin go? I was like a lone leaf afloat in a vast ocean. Wandering the streets, I lied about my age and enlisted in the military. In wartime, such things were possible. Jiae, you don't know what war is, what death means. At that age, I experienced everything one might in a lifetime. War is ugly, and human life can be so trivial."

He casually kicked a fallen leaf at his feet, watching it rustle away into the distance. They were alone in the campus grounds.

"I despaired seeing the stark reality of humans, worse than may-flies, in a civil war. I escaped from a war where I didn't even know whom I was fighting for. Deserting the military was simple then. One day, during an operation to climb a hill, I was at the very back, and I seized the chance to escape. Disguised as a beggar, I made my way to Busan. There, I sold the ring my mother had given me and started a small street business. At night, I attended night school. That's where I became friends with an American officer. We've maintained our friendship to this day, and it was with his help that I eventually came to study in the U.S."

His story lingered, tugging at her heartstrings. This isn't it, this isn't it... But the beckoning hand of adventurous youth waved at her. Could she trust him? She shook her head.

As Thanksgiving approached, he suggested a weekend outing nearby, and Jiae, having just completed a burdensome assignment and feeling relieved, readily agreed.

"Not far from here, there's a folk museum in the mountains. It houses many artifacts from the Native Americans and the Civil War era.""

"Side by side, they settled into their seats on the bus. He was visibly excited, like a primary school student on a field trip. Jiae's spirits were lifted by the long-missed view of the outdoors.

"Ah, such a beautiful world!" Jiae couldn't tear her eyes away from the lush trees and the splendid display of autumn leaves. The vast, serene rural landscapes of America and the tall, straight pine trees lining the highway mesmerized her, making her feel like she was traversing a fairytale.

"Being outside with you, Jiae, reminds me of the seagulls by the Daedong River. After school, I used to go up to Moran Hill with my friends. The seagulls would fly right up to us, flapping their wings and cawing. When I think of 'home,' I picture the Daedong River and the seagulls of Moran Hill. And in spring, the hill would be blanketed with azaleas. It's been said that azaleas are the soul of our people. The way they bloom so generously, the azalea forests on Moran Hill spoke of our nation's generosity and courage."

His eyes held a distant glow.

"The simplicity and passion of the azaleas, maybe that's why we have so many poets and artists."

Jiae added,

"The more troubled and impoverished the country, the more artists it seems to have."

A faint mist seemed to form in his eyes as he gazed out the bus window. Right in front of them, a squirrel played on the marble floor beneath an oak tree, like water droplets dancing. It suddenly stopped and looked at them, its eyes rolling in surprise. Jiae laughed at the cute gaze of the squirrel, but as he moved closer to her, she shifted away, and the startled squirrel scampered up the tree. The sound of birds from the tree the squirrel climbed evoked memories, like echoes from the past.

She thought of her hometown.

Houses huddled together against a gently sloping hill, with a river flowing from the mountain in front. Yes, the well was the gathering place for the women of the village. Sitting with knees on the broad, smooth stone floor, they would prepare vegetables or wash rice for dinner, while the news of the neighborhood fluttered from mouth to mouth. Does that hometown still exist? Untouched by time, with the river, the well, and the neighborly love still intact, standing resilient against the winds of rural exodus?

The murmuring of tourists visiting the folk museum reached their ears. The rustling of fallen leaves on the flat ground where they sat surrounded by layers of trees and shrubs sounded like the rumbling of waves under the sea. Among the mostly white tourists, Jiae felt a kinship not with the war-related artifacts from the Civil War but with the rusty, crude equipment and the oil-stained, gleaming looms."

"Sitting side by side on the bus, they were engrossed in the view outside. A Puritan woman with a white towel on her head was mimicking the act of spinning yarn on the loom. Despite modern times bringing East and West closer, Jiae felt that in the relics of the past, buried in the tomb of time, the world seemed to share a common root.

"This place is so peaceful. The air is fresh in the mountains, and it brings clarity to the mind," he mused dreamily, then turned to look at Jiae. "Jiae, I was really worried you'd reject me. It's been a tough month, especially with my thesis writing."

Before she could respond, he suddenly slid closer and enveloped her in an embrace. "Oh no, you shouldn't do this!" She hadn't expected this, had not followed him for this. Jiae struggled to free herself from his grip. "Jiae, I love you. Ever since I first saw you on campus, I've always…"

Was this how a starving beast behaved? He pressed her against his chest, making it hard for her to breathe. Suddenly, he seemed frightening, but his hold was unyielding. She felt utterly defeated in this struggle. A chilly autumn breeze caressed her bare skin. Like a child coloring outside the lines, her protected world was violently torn apart. Tears welled up in Jiae's eyes – tears of injustice, shame, and humiliation.

In a distant, foggy hill in her hometown, a young girl, unaware of the situation, clutched her disheveled clothes. The face of her mother overlapped with that of the girl adjusting her clothes. The girl sat by the river, washing clothes. Jiae sat silently, a distance away from him, her head buried between her knees. The basket that once held colorful flowers was now empty… Where was her picture book? Hyun's face came to mind, his expression pained.

"I'm sorry. Please forgive me. We are destined…" His voice feigned tenderness as he reached to wrap his arm around her shoulder, but it felt foreign to her. "We'll get married soon. That will solve everything."

His voice grew urgent. "Jiae, I want to know what happiness is, do you understand? I want to be happy. Happiness, just happiness. We can be happy."

Was he crying? His shoulders shook as he bowed his head. "A woman should always be mindful of her conduct..." It was as if her mother was speaking right beside her. Jiae felt a pang of pain in her body. As he reached out to embrace her again, she pushed him away and sprang up, running through the shrubs. "Jiae!" He called her name, following her.

The following spring, as Park Jaehoon awaited his degree after his thesis was approved, he decided to stay at his alma mater until Jiae completed her graduation thesis. Working as a research assistant with the professors, they eventually had a simple ceremony at the dean's house on the night of the Christmas festival."

"Subtitle: New York

"Oh my, this place is like a showcase of races!"

Jiae marveled inwardly. On the streets and in department stores, there were Caucasians, African Americans, and people from South America who resembled Koreans... In the heart of New York, where clothing style seemed a secondary concern, everyone appeared as free and comfortable as if they were in their own homes, born and raised here, living their entire lives in this city.

Above all, Jiae was pleased to frequently see faces of fellow Koreans.

As life in New York stabilized and the initial excitement subsided, Jiae began to see another side of the city. The streets were dirty, and there was a pervasive sense of individualism, indifference, and especially, the subtle tension of having to navigate around the white population who acted as if they owned the place. The so-called latecomers had to squeeze their way in, finding a space to breathe.

"It's just that they arrived earlier, and we came later..." Whenever such thoughts crossed her mind, Jiae felt a sense of injustice. After all, wasn't this a land where everyone was a guest, with no true owners?"

"After her husband left for work and her son for school, Jiae often found herself wandering the streets of Manhattan alone, her heart filled with an unquenchable restlessness and thirst, as though she were strolling through the bustling streets of Myeongdong or Taepyeong-ro in Seoul. One day, while she stood watching an elderly man feeding pigeons in front of the public library, she heard a voice exclaim,

"Oh my, isn't that Jiae?"

Startled, she turned to see who it was.

"Oh my!"

15

It was Miyoung, a familiar face, her expression a mix of surprise and delight.

"Can it be? Are you not Miyoung?"

"Yes, it's unbelievable!"

"To think we'd meet here of all places!"

The two embraced, then clasped hands and shook them, unable to contain their excitement.

"You haven't changed a bit, you know!"

"Neither have you... It's like a dream!"

They hugged again, heedless of the passersby, their heels clicking in excitement.

"Wandering these streets, it's no wonder we bumped into each other."

Miyoung's eyes darted between the white and the pupil as she looked at Jiae. "Are you just loafing around?"

"What?"

"Well, actually, I've just moved here from another state not long ago."

"Is that so? Are you looking for work? The hospital where I work is looking for a social worker. It's right up your alley since you majored in the same field. And I bet your English is just fine."

Miyoung, who had been close friends with Jiae since high school and kept in touch until Jiae got married, had been in the US for five years, recently completing her medical exams and now working as an intern.

"It would be great to work together, just like old times, seeing each other every day."

"It really would be wonderful. Meeting you here, it almost feels like Seoul. You even bring the scent of Seoul with you."

"Oh, you're still the same. Always so refreshing."

"Not really, you know."

Jiae playfully tapped Miyoung's shoulder, her mood momentarily turning glum. As they sat side by side in front of the library, chatting away, even the old man feeding the pigeons couldn't help but glance over and chuckle. A flock of pigeons pecked at the feed, busily circling around.

"I actually came here to meet someone during my lunch break."
Releasing each other's hands, Miyoung stood up.

"I'll be in touch soon."

"Yes, let's meet again."

Jiae watched Miyoung's retreating figure for a while before turning away. A sudden desire to work too welled up deep inside her."

"The shock that Jiae felt was like a forgotten spring grass suddenly stirring... In that moment, the expressionless face of her husband also flashed in her mind. He probably wouldn't object.

That night, after returning from the hospital lab and while having dinner, she casually mentioned meeting Miyoung and her intention to work. Observing her husband's silent sighs, she decided to call Miyoung the next day.

"Don't worry. I've already spoken about it. It's almost as if you're already hired. I didn't think your husband would oppose. And if he does, just kick away his objections and run off. Ha, haha... I've changed a lot, haven't I? How come you're still the same? You really haven't changed. That's why I like you, I guess."

"Divorce, the culmination of life? No, it's defeat, the absolute end," Julie, contrary to the vibe her name suggested, mused with her plump body swaying in self-derision. "Even so, I was slim when I was with my husband."

In a society where being overweight is seen as a major disgrace for women, she blamed her weight gain entirely on her divorce. Jiae wasn't sure if that was true, but the young woman in the old photos Julie showed was indeed different. "Divorce is the end of life? Julie, you don't seem like the other women here."

"It's madness, utter madness. Who in their right mind would get a divorce?"

"Julie, look for a job."

"Tch, why work? Who would pay me to work? Would you give someone like me a job? That's absurd."

"There are plenty of volunteer opportunities, you know? Our hospital is always open to volunteers. You need something to devote yourself to, passionately. You don't need medication."

"Ha, then I should fall in love. Jiae, could you introduce me to a Korean man? Just one person would do. Ha, ho-ho."

She burst into laughter and pulled a handkerchief from her handbag to dab at her eyes.

Jiae felt despair watching her.

"Julie, you must think I'm joking."

"Well, I know. But I've never worked outside in my life."

Julie quickly reined in her laughter, her expression turning gloomy as she looked out the window. "That's why you should start. Julie, don't you want to be beautiful again? You can regain your youthful appearance."

Jiae wanted to uplift her, this woman discarded by a man, like a rotten log.

"But I'm just too heavy."

She bowed her head, not wanting to say more. Without any children to care for, she was living aimlessly on the alimony her ex-husband sent every month."

"As Jiae's chronic stomach issues led her to frequent hospital visits, the attending physician assigned her to counsel Julie. The words Julie carelessly uttered, 'Divorce is the end of life,' stuck in Jiae's throat like a thorn. Why would she say that? Suddenly, Jiae's husband's face came to mind. Lately, he had become even more reticent, and she didn't know why. Could there be some unavoidable issue at work? Had he grown to dislike New York? If he didn't like it here, where should they go? Where had the bluebird of happiness he once fervently spoke of on that Appalachian hill gone? 'Happiness, happiness, we will find happiness,' he had said, but now all she could do was sigh.

"Is something bothering you? What's wrong?"

Julie peered at her cautiously.

"No, it's nothing... just a bit tired, no, it's nothing really."

"Well, I should be going then. I don't want to tire you out with my boring stories."

Julie heaved her hefty frame up with difficulty, winked one eye, and left the office. Jiae moved to the window, feeling gloomy. The sky was overcast as usual, with dull sunlight bathing the hospital's backyard.

Spring was on its way.

Through the forsythia forest pathway, she could see an elderly Caucasian lady, seemingly in her sixties, pushing a wheelchair. Her husband sat in it, chatting and laughing with her as they passed by, likely heading to the park on the premises. Their affectionate demeanor made Jiae reflect on her relationship with her husband.

Why does he seem to be shutting me out? He has become more despondent recently.

Why can't we be just normal? Maybe not happy but...

Could something have happened at work? Or was it the news from North Korea? She remembered how, right after coming to New York, he had cheerfully chatted with Professor K, who lived with an American woman. He had been eager to taste kimchi, praising North Korea for days. That was a side of him she had never seen. But after that, Professor K disappeared without a trace.

Since then, her husband's gloominess had noticeably deepened. He constantly sighed, and his eyes seemed always to be looking inward. Was it the stress from work, spreading like silent, toxic mushrooms into their home? He wouldn't even open up to their only son.

A memory of his words came back to her. Typically quiet at home, he had suddenly spoken up one evening during dinner.

"I had a big fight with the hospital director today. Always calling me in, but...""

""What was the reason?" Jiae inquired.

"It's simple. They claim my research didn't uncover anything new. Of course, that's just an excuse."

"Why would they do that?"

"It's a signal for me to leave. They're reluctant to promote me to a permanent position, especially since I come from a small country in the East. They're hesitant to make someone like me a permanent staff member." Jiae, not wanting to upset him further, remained silent. He hesitated, then spoke as if chewing on unfinished thoughts.

"By the way, I got a call from a university in Seoul. They're inviting me to join them. Should I go? Our son, Jaesik, will be going to college soon anyway..."

"...?"

"What do you think?" He looked intently at her, seemingly urging her to respond. Jiae met his gaze. Was this the inevitable finally happening? He didn't propose they leave together. Of course, even if he had suggested it, she wouldn't go.

"Stay for another three years..."

"Do that," Jiae replied, her voice weak, like a sick cat dragging its tail.

A month later, he left. Waving back at the airport terminal, he looked almost like a schoolboy off to a field trip.

At that moment, Jiae felt grateful for him, for not insisting on going to North Korea... There had been a time after their marriage when he subtly hinted at moving there. How shocked and anxious she had been then.

On her way home from work, Jiae stopped by a children's arcade. It was a place she visited when not too busy or when feeling a bit empty.

"Stop, stop, buddy!"

In the arcade, about five or six kids were each engrossed in their games, seated in electric chairs.

Seeing Jiae, Jack approached and hugged her.

"Oh, Jack, how have you been?"

"Good. I missed you, Jiae."

Just then, Julie entered, her face pale as if she had never seen sunlight, holding the wrist of a child with a radiant smile.

"Hi, Jiae!"

Jiae looked at Julie with satisfaction. Julie, once like a tree grown only in the shade, damp and full of complaints, had heeded her advice and had been volunteering at the children's ward for two years now. She still received regular living expenses from her ex-husband. While her plump figure hadn't changed, the aura around her was entirely different. She radiated vitality and warmth. That's the scent of life, Jiae thought, feeling a sense of fulfillment from seeing Julie."

""Guess what."

Jack's blue eyes sparkled as he looked at Jiae, winking one eye playfully.

"What is it? Tell me, Jack."

"The doctor said I can go home this Christmas. Mom's planning to throw a big party and invite lots of friends."

"That sounds wonderful, Jack. You've got a fantastic plan."

"This Christmas, I'm going to pray that Jiae meets the person she most wants to see in the world."

Then, innocently, he clasped his hands in front of his chest and mimicked the act of praying.

"Thank you, Jack. I really hope that happens too."

Her own words unexpectedly brought tears to her eyes. Why am I feeling this way? Is New York too desolate for me? Like a sack full of grain, so full that even a slight press makes the seeds burst out, spilling my longing. Jack lowered his hands and smiled shyly.

"Ah, that smile!"

Jiae was taken aback and stared at the boy.

Over Jack's innocent smile, she saw Hyun's smile superimposed. She suddenly longed to see him. "Jiae, you should be happy." His voice, fresh like cabbage just salted for kimchi, bubbled somewhere in her heart.

Where might he be now, under which slice of sky?"

"Subtitle: Ah, A Korean

That day, Jiae set out to Broadway Avenue to prepare Christmas gifts for Jack and her colleagues at work. Her son, who had gone to Boston University three years ago, was also coming for Christmas. The festive mood of the season was in full swing, with Christmas carols echoing from every store, lifting the spirits of the passersby. Santa Claus, dressed in a bizarre costume as if part of a strange masquerade, was approaching from the other end of the alley. The arrival of the year's end transformed the streets into an unreal realm, as if revamping them into a tale from a distant past, a legend devoid of war or hatred.

The emotions she felt during this season were always the same. Ever since her mother passed away, the festivities in America felt more like somber memorial days, tinged with gray, leaving her lonelier and more forlorn. As she walked with her head bowed, a Salvation Army officer wearing a red hat rang his bell with a clanging sound. Moved by the chime, she took out $10 from her wallet and dropped it into the red kettle hanging from the tripod."

"As Jiae zipped up her handbag and turned around, her gaze fell upon a wave of people in the distance. Among them, a familiar face was approaching her. As the distance closed, the face broke into a broad grin.

"My, what a surprise to see you here, Jiae!"

"Oh, Min-guk Sim!"

Suddenly, a scent of lilacs wafted through the air like a mist, lighting a lantern somewhere in her heart. Memories of May on the university campus, the sun-drenched library, and piles of crimson leaves at the corner of the building flooded her mind.

"Goodness, to run into you like this, ha ha."

His face was a bloom of smiles.

"Really, it's so good to see you. Heh heh."

Jiae was delighted. "Meeting a university classmate here!"

Mr. Sim ushered Jiae towards a nearby coffee shop.

"Jiae, I mean, that might be inappropriate now. You must be a proud Mrs. by now."

"It's okay, you can call me anything. I've become Mrs. Park."

"Ah, I see. Ha ha."

He laughed heartily and ordered two cups of coffee.

"But Mrs. Park, you seem just like you always were, not a bit changed."

"Not at all. I've changed a lot."

There was a hollowness in Jiae's voice. 'Hyun, if only we could meet like this too...' A fleeting rumor that Hyun had been in New York once crossed her mind. She hadn't believed it then. And she couldn't ask this man about him. Mr. Sim's face, slightly swollen like damp bread, seemed to overlay with Hyun's face like a projection on a screen.

"What does your husband do?"

"Pardon?"

"Your husband. What does he do?"

"Oh, him? He's currently in Korea."

"Is that so?"

His skeptical look made her uncomfortable. He averted his gaze and changed the topic.

"The world is really a strange place. Men grow wrinkles every day, and flesh keeps piling up like this, while women... it's as if they've eaten the elixir of Emperor Qin Shi Huang or something..."

"Maybe it's not that, maybe men are just too greedy?"

Jiae replied playfully, with a twinkle in her eye.

"Ha ha, it's not so much greed as it is a struggle. A struggle with oneself, with family, with societal responsibilities and duties, that sort of thing. The world of men is not simple. Jiae, do I look much older?"

"Well, I recognized you right away, didn't I?""

"Jiae cracked a faint smile. Maybe men do age faster and change like he said. Had Hyun changed too, becoming worldly like this?

"When did you come to the US?" Mr. Sim threw the casual question that's almost like a morning greeting in New York.

"Pardon?"

"I mean, when did you come to America?"

"It's been a long time for me. How about you?"

"Me? Oh, nothing extraordinary. Caught up in marriage, harried by kids, henpecked by the wife, and now shamelessly seated here. I haven't been in the US for long. I'm here on a business assignment. How much longer I'll stay or if I'll settle down here... well, that's up in the air, especially considering the kids..."

He trailed off, a bitter taste in his mouth. The coffee had gone cold. He quickly gulped down his lukewarm cup.

"Oh dear, the coffee's gone cold. Let's order another. I'll have one more."

Jiae waved her hand.

"No, don't order for me. I actually can't have coffee in the evening."

"Then you must have some juice. We can't just meet like this and have just a cup of coffee and juice."

Without asking Jiae, he ordered orange juice. Jiae chuckled as she watched him. Ah, he's a typical Korean man, acting on his own accord, thinking that's what women like...

Pines came to her mind. Tall pines on the hill, their fragrance wafting through the air with the rustling sound of stream water whenever the wind blew. Ah, Korean men, always be so pleasantly unchanged. Remain evergreen, born and raised in a small country, coming here with an iron will, chasing dreams with unwavering spirit, the staunch men of South Korea.

"Thank you."

Jiae sipped her juice through a straw.

"What do you do? You seem to be on your way from work. I apologize, your family must be waiting at home."

Jiae thought to herself, 'No one's waiting for me at home.' But she replied,

"It's fine. I've got some time this evening. See, I came out for shopping."

"Ah, I see!"

Mr. Sim didn't inquire further.

The coffee shop was growing quieter. Here, unlike hanging out with colleagues after work, men often headed straight home - a simple reason for their routine. They endure the office grind during the day and seek the comfort of their cozy homes, their 'sweet home' awaiting them at night. Even in America, this traditional pattern is crumbling, especially in large cities where more women are entering professional fields, and couples are working outside together.

Cities like New York are changing even faster. Along with these changes, the traditional family bonds are also weakening. Can money ever recover what's precious but lost in this shift?"

""Shouldn't you be heading home?" Jiae cautiously asked.

"No, not yet."

His face contorted as if biting into a sour fruit.

"Really, the community spirit among the Korean expats here seems to be getting harsher. Everyone's possessed by the drive to make money. It's good to work hard to make a good life in this strange land, but it's becoming too cutthroat."

It was as if a dam of pent-up thoughts had burst. His voice rose passionately.

"It's fine to earn money... but the problem is the attitude of throwing away the old like worn-out clothes, things we cherished back in our homeland. Isn't it 'jeong' above all? Koreans are Koreans wherever they go. We shouldn't forget that jeong. I believe it's a unique part of our culture. Jeong can't be properly translated into English or any other language."

"Yes, I agree that jeong is our unique culture," Jiae found herself getting drawn into the conversation.

"Indeed. I still long for the old-time warmth and kindness of the folks back in the countryside."

"Well, maybe it's because we've been repressed for so long, living lives determined by others... No, I'm thinking this: maybe it's because we're still in the early stages of immigration. Everything is unstable, the situation is uncertain, and that's why it's like this? The easy money is appealing, and there's greed to make a fortune."

"The problem is the growing children, our future. Just as a house needs a strong and straight main beam, children are that main beam, aren't they? It's true we're in the early stages of immigration, and that's why these things happen. But what will become of these neglected children as they grow? I agree, money is good, but I can't agree with the notion that we shouldn't worry too much about the growing children."

"Don't misunderstand me. But I believe we will get a grip on this soon. Is there any other nation as resilient as ours, South Korea? We're a people with a spirit that knows how to navigate through thorny paths. Initially, there might be chaos, but we quickly straighten things out."

"Of course, you're right. But one thing I've realized since coming to America is that people should live comfortably, at least not beholden to the gaze of others, if not entirely by free will. That's freedom and happiness. My own theory of freedom and happiness, haha.""

""Is that a decadent philosopher's pragmatic view of reality? Or... Heh." Jiae joined in the laughter. 'Yes, he used to be quite serious back then,' she thought, as she changed her tone.

"Sir, I believe that when our immigrant community stabilizes, we will bloom here, drawing on our strengths. Once we're more settled, our jeong will surely flourish. Our intelligence, artistic nature, and ambition will blossom. Right now, we're in the process of putting down roots. The important thing is how we envision our tomorrow, isn't it?"

"Indeed."

"The issue is how we view what's wrong at present. That's where we must start."

Jiae's eyes seemed to dream. Mr. Sim looked at her, astonished. Jiae, changing her tone and growing impassioned, continued,

"Someday, we too will shine. Then the world will say, 'Look at those Koreans,' and gaze at us with admiration. That day will come when we can spread our wings. As I said, the current irregularities might just be inevitable bumps in the road during our settlement phase."

"Wow, Jiae, that's impressive!"

He opened his mouth wide and grasped Jiae's hand, which she shyly smiled at.

"But you know, a few days ago, I happened to meet a colleague from Seoul on the street. I was so happy that I instinctively reached out to greet him. But he momentarily flashed a look of recognition, then suddenly disappeared into the crowd. I was dumbfounded and just stared at his retreating figure. I even called out his name, thinking I might have been mistaken. I guessed he wanted to avoid me because of his unkempt hair and shabby work clothes, but it was really bitter."

"Yes, indeed. In a place where there's no distinction in jobs, what's there to shy away from?"

"What saddens me is the lack of pride. Don't we have the blood of the first generation of immigrants who toiled in the pineapple fields of Hawaii, whose perseverance and sincerity flow through us? That's our strength to survive in America. Of course, transitional phenomena are natural."

Jiae spoke with conviction, supporting his words.

"I see America as a truly charming place. Newcomers can fit into mainstream society without abandoning their identity, just by finding the right angle."

"That's a very apt observation. The same nation that preserved the thousand-year history of Chinese pottery as its own, that adapted ginseng to our soil to make it a world-renowned product, all these are our people's achievements, aren't they?'"

"This can be considered a fine example of cultural fusion," he said. "Yes, indeed, it's truly about cultural integration," Ji-ae responded, finding her previously stifled mood significantly lightened during their conversation. "I had such a great time today. It feels good to be able to speak so freely." It was heartfelt. "I feel the same. Meeting an old classmate in New York and being able to share inner thoughts... Today feels special, almost like it's my birthday. But

I've probably been babbling too much, haven't I? Meeting Ji-ae made me so excited; it's as if I've returned to the past..."

"I felt that way too. It's really nice to talk about deep, personal things." It truly was. Such thoughts crept in again, wondering if it was possible to meet Hyun like this. His presence seemed both obstinate like a child who refuses to be erased from a distant memory and hesitant like a child without confidence, carrying an incomplete homework notebook to school.

"Ha-ha, I see. So that's the good thing about having classmates. Speaking of classmates... I almost forgot." He took out his notebook to check a place and date written there. "There's an upcoming alumni reunion. You should come, Ji-ae. If transportation is an issue, I'd be happy to take you. My wife will be coming along as well."

"Sure."

"I'll definitely make it out that day, no matter how busy I am. The world of careers is truly daunting. Even if I wanted to change my career now, it would be difficult. I'll give you a call that day," he said, checking the phone number Ji-ae had given him. His business card stated he was the representative of the Korean-American Trade Association branch in New York. After parting with him, she suddenly felt an emptiness inside her. It was as if she was standing in front of a movie screen, transitioning from a vibrant scene to a dark one. Was it because she had shared too much? As if already enveloped in darkness, the prematurely setting winter sun had disappeared beyond the forest of the Empire State Building, and a rather chilly air had begun to circulate on the streets. She had intended to head to the subway station, shielding herself with her thin coat, but instead, she decided to hail a taxi. She didn't want to see or meet anyone. The taxi came to a stop in front of her. "Where to?" asked the young Spanish driver, turning to look at Ji-ae. "Flushing." "Okay!" The driver glanced at her through the rearview mirror and flashed a smile. "Ah, you're Chinese?" "No, I am Korean," Ji-ae responded, feeling unnecessarily irritated by that all-too-familiar assumption.

"Oh, never mind, never mind," said the driver, turning up the radio.

You are my sunshine,
My only sunshine.
When the gray clouds cover the sky,
You make me happy.
Please, just leave my sunshine be.

The deep, settled voice of a black female singer began to fill the car, like a stream flowing through parched land.

Even though the world is dark and rough,
Please give me a coat of many colors.
A lovely coat of many colors.
I will engrave my dreams on the brilliant coat.
I will embrace you with my dreams.
Please, please give me a coat of many colors.

Ji-ae thought of the music room she left behind in Korea. A place with the scent of fragrant coffee, where classical music quietly flowed and youth resided. Even after living in the US for a long time, the places she missed were like that. No matter where she went in America,

There was a place imbued with a uniquely Korean ambiance, filled with a warmth and romance that could only be found in Korea, a location where the distinctive affection and spirit of Korea prevailed. Those youthful days were overwhelmingly vibrant. Regardless of the era or place, youth pressed down with an unbearable weight, yet how philosophical it was. Despair sweetly nurtured our dreams, sanctified our youth, and provided strength. In smoke-filled rooms, we surrendered ourselves to music, appearing gloomy as if we had become poisonous mushrooRather than going to the mountains for romantic escapades, we, like today's youth who might indulge in opium or alcohol, were intoxicated by Tchaikovsky, Brahms, Wagner. Yes, I too suffered from love. My beloved was a philosophy student from the same school, notably tall with an impeccable stride. He was a person of deep thought and clear judgment, possessing both the laughter of an old man and a boy. Still, he remains the eternal spring in my soul. Perhaps, that too is metaphysical? My love for him as well. As we approached the Queensboro Bridge, the traffic began to crawl. Both routes to Manhattan and Queens were congested. A state mental hospital stood in the middle of the East River bank against a gloomy, leaden sky. Those within the asylum, believing themselves to be kings and princesses, might be the only truly happy individuals on earth, living happily in an imagined, unreal world. Ji-ae, oddly enough, found it amusing to empathize with them, to become them in her thoughts. "Traffic, traffic."

The driver grumbled. Why did Hyun give up on becoming a nun? Ji-ae heard rumors right before she left that Hyun had abandoned her plans to study in Germany for nun training. This unfinished task in life was still holding her back.

Two Men

The car crawled along. The sullen face of her husband flashed through her mind. It had been three years since his last return home, and he had suddenly appeared only to leave again after a week. On the evening before his departure, he had finally spoken up. "There was a girl I promised my future to during high school. After I left, she ventured alone to the south in search of me. Imagine, all those long years. By chance, as I was walking in Myeong-dong, amidst the crowd, she was approaching me. Her long straight hair still fluttered over her shoulders, and that woman with the long legs and pale face was coming towards me. Once she reached me, without a hint of shyness, she abruptly grabbed my hand and started crying." Silence followed. Ji-ae broke the awkward silence, "It was that woman, wasn't it?" He glanced at her briefly, as if wondering how she knew. "Yes," he confirmed.

To Ji-ae, his "Yes" sounded like that of a confessor before a priest. "Indeed, that woman... she didn't marry and only waited for me, wandering aimlessly," he exhaled deeply. "Her tears pressed on me more than joy. Her face retained its youthful beauty, but the palms holding my hands were as hard as stone. It eloquently spoke of the rough life she had endured. I surrendered to those hands." "So, you ended up living together," Ji-ae cut in nonchalantly. "......What I really need to confess is that my returning to Korea was also to see her. I heard rumors she was somewhere in Seoul." Ah, so that was it. He glanced at Ji-ae, as if gauging her reaction. "I'm sorry." There was no change in Ji-ae's expression. "She had been updating me about our home over the years. My siblings went to China, and my mother stayed home alone, daily gazing at the southern sky, hands clasped over her chest," his eyes reddened as if touched by the sunset. "Our living together was inevitable......"

"Stop, you don't need to make excuses," Ji-ae waved her hand. "It's not an excuse..." "It's okay. You don't need to worry about me............" Did I feel betrayed by him, trying to find an escape? At that moment, she diverted her thoughts to the bench in front of the university library. She heard the rustling sound of stepping on fallen leaves. Hyun was standing right next to her. Against the backdrop of the burning red sunset over the medical school's forest, his laughter in the twilight was fading into the shadows. Then and now. "Some people go back and forth across the Han River, from North to South," he said, almost to himself, snapping her back to reality. What was he trying to say? A stone seemed to hit Ji-ae's heart with a thud. He closed his mouth. His sealed lips resembled the firmly shut iron gates of a forsaken dynasty. Ji-ae remembered his words on that hill near DongSan Apartment complex, "This is fate," and after marriage, "What if we go North?" Ah, why is he like this? What made this man, with his brilliant mind and top-notch education, become such a powerless escapist, lacking confidence in life and resorting to excuses...

"Some say they can cross back and forth along the Han River, between the North and the South," he uttered almost to himself, the last remark clinging to her heart like some adhesive. 'So, what is he implying?' Suspicion and pity filled Ji-ae's eyes as she looked at him. The next day, refusing Ji-ae's offer to drive him to the airport and calling a taxi instead, he repeated his apologies. As they stood at the door, he took Ji-ae's hands for a moment, his eyes moist. Are you now happy? Have you found the happiness you so desired? Ji-ae asked him silently, her hand still in his. His cheek twitched slightly as if to smile. "Please, speak kindly of me to Jae-sik." What did he mean by telling Jae-sik? Ji-ae watched the back wheels of his departing taxi with an uncertain heart. Nothing was clear. He left as if only shrouding everything under a dense fog of irresponsibility. Why did he come? It couldn't have been just to relay that woman's message... Then what? The word 'divorce' briefly surfaced like a bubble before sinking away. Maybe that was it. But why did he just go back as he came? Ji-ae felt a confusing and strange premonition that he would never return. Poor man!

The day Ji-ae first followed her friend, it coincided with Hyun's book presentation day. "Ji-ae, pay close attention to that guy. He's an exceptional brain. Despite numerous female students flocking to him, he shows no interest. Try your hand at it. Let's see your prowess, hehe." "You see..." Ji-ae strangely didn't find him unfamiliar at her first encounter. Speaking in front of about ten male and female college students, he wasn't flustered or exaggerated but spoke methodically with a smile, which irresistibly drew Ji-ae in. It felt surreal, as though she had met him once in a past where everything was vague and shrouded in fog. Yes, he was interpreting Kierkegaard's philosophy, 'Beyond Despair'. For the first time, Ji-ae learned that this philosopher posited that humans find God within the abyss of despair. "Kierkegaard aimed to resolve the nihilism and despair of existentialism with the light from beyond. In a way, he attempted a rebirth of new humanity there," he said. His voice seemed to carry the distant sound of water flowing through a mountain ravine on the wind. After the meeting, ignoring her friend's offer to introduce him, Ji-ae quickly left the spot. She then attended that gathering every week thereafter. They would invite renowned speakers for lectures, or one of the participating students would present on a book they had read.

When there was neither this nor that to discuss, they simply sat around and debated various topics, sharing their views. That day, Ji-ae was sitting on a long bench next to the library, gazing at the twilight that was blazing red. It was like a fire. A flame that thoroughly rummaged through the depths of the human psyche, vividly exposing agony and solitude, pulling her in like a suction plate, absorbing everything around her. Then, Ji-ae heard footsteps approaching nearby and turned her head. He was standing there, seemingly having just come out of the library. "May I sit here?" "Yes," she answered, somewhat taken aback. "You've stayed late at school." "Yes, the twilight is just too beautiful." Unexpectedly, those words escaped Ji-ae's lips. For a while, they silently gave their attention to the burning sunset. "Let's go," he eventually said as he got up. Ji-ae rose as if drawn by a magnet. Side by side, they left the campus, walking through the college streets. The evening was sweeping the darkness away with an invisible broom. At a fork in the road, he waved goodbye. After parting ways with him, Ji-ae almost ran back home.

"Hey, it's late," her mother emerged from the master bedroom, examining her face. "I was at the library..." Ji-ae stumbled over her words. "Are you unwell? Why does your complexion look like that?" "No, Mom. Maybe because I ran here." "Child, have some warm tea first." Her mother's quiet and worried voice came from outside the door. When Ji-ae opened the door, she first noticed her mother's bare feet. Entering, her mother placed a cup of tea down, stood momentarily, then said, "Let's have dinner soon," before leaving. Ji-ae watched her mother's neatly pinned hair from the back as she turned to leave, feeling a lump in her throat. Her mother, who had never shown a disheveled appearance, watches over her only daughter's every move, even the minutest movements of her heart, without missing a single thread. She sifts through words like picking pebbles out of sand, choosing her words carefully, never uttering a word in vain. Even in times apart from her mother, Ji-ae could never escape her mother's quiet gaze and her silent words. Would her mother understand the heart of her daughter, who is suffering from love? She scolded herself internally. She ought to focus solely on her studies for her mother's sake... Yet, soon she will graduate and leave for America. How will her mother live alone? How much time had passed since then? That day, too, Ji-ae left the library and headed home.

Before leaving, Ji-ae was sitting on a bench at a corner of the schoolyard. The corners of the yard were filled with leaves piling up among the grass and bushes. Occasionally, the early winter wind would carry the leaves, rustling as they scattered. The melancholy of Verlaine, which she had been reciting just moments ago, and the sighs of the leaves were still sobbing in a corner of her heart. To divert her mind, Ji-ae softly recited Paul Claudel's "Cantata". He hears the sound of the people marching from behind in the mist, and now he sees the sun, risen to the height of his knees like a blush of rose on linen. Now the mist thins, and suddenly, the entire promised land appears to his eyes in brilliant light, like a virgin, dripping with water

droplets and lushly green, as if a woman has just emerged from bath-
ing. Unbeknownst to her when he arrived, he was right next to her.

"You're still here. It's nice to see you." Ji-ae was surprised, her
skirt fluttering as she quickly stood up. "Please, have a seat." His gaze
into her eyes was piercing, his voice carrying the scent of iris leaves.
Ji-ae sat back down, her heart fluttering. Ah, why do I feel this way?
She clenched her knees together. "The weather is getting colder," he
remarked. "Yes, winter is upon us." "This winter will be the last one,"
he said. "Yes, it will," Ji-ae responded, looking back at him. "Do you
have any plans?" "I'm not sure yet. Maybe I'll go to America." "Ah,
I see." Their eyes met. "I heard you're going to Germany." "Perhaps
I will." There was a hint of uncertainty in his voice. "...Is there a
change in your decision?" She knew that after his graduation, he was
supposed to go to Germany to become a priest.

"Do you have time, Ji-ae?" he suddenly asked with effort. "If
you do, I was thinking of buying you a coffee." "I have time," of
course, for you, anytime, as much as needed... Ji-ae stood up, fol-
lowing him. His back, with hands deeply buried in his coat pockets,
walking away, pained her. The topic he presented at a recent meet-
ing flashed through her mind—about Heidegger and Nietzsche, she
wanted to know what tormented and bewildered him. He stopped,
turned around, and walked alongside Ji-ae. The twilight tangled
down on the lake's surface without a single breeze, cold mist licking
at their necks. The plane trees darkened, leaves falling one by one,
then in bunches, scattering everywhere, rolling together as if danc-
ing, then parting. Is lack of purpose natural? "Humans and animals
meet in plants and vegetation." Such a thought suddenly crossed
Ji-ae's mind. "Ji-ae, have you ever seen death?" he turned to her. "Yes,
when I was in the first grade of elementary school, the child of a lady
who lived with us died of a fever."

My mom and the lady would take turns holding the child on
their laps, but one day, I saw the baby laid on the floor, covered
entirely with a white cloth, even over the face." "Ah, I see." "And
then, after a while, I witnessed my grandfather pass away. He was
over eighty years old and passed away so peacefully, as if he knew it
was his time, just like falling asleep. He was a pastor. He was inspired

and became a pastor after working with an American missionary, despite coming from a Confucian family." "Truly like a leaf gently falling," he remarked, almost sighing. "Yes, that's right. He left this world so purely. He said, 'I am going to my Father,' and then he quietly closed his eyes. My grandmother tightly shut her eyes and wiped her tears with a handkerchief, but there was an indescribable, fragrant aura floating around the room." "Your grandfather didn't just experience death. He fought with the angel of death with his faith and won. In a way, his death was another beginning, a change in the form of life, perhaps." "Is that so?" "Yes. He went to the country he longed for. Ji-ae, the death I witnessed was entirely different." "Who was it?" "It was my father."

"I'm sorry for bringing that up." "It's okay. I was actually about to tell you about it." They sat in a corner of the only cafe nestled within the university's forest. "Shall we have some coffee?" Two cups of coffee were placed before them. As Tchaikovsky's Symphony No. 5 concluded, Mendelssohn's String Quartet softly filled the air. "My father was a resister." "…?" "He was a student who opposed the Japanese colonial policies. Going to study in Tokyo. Back then, for Korean youth, it was considered the most prestigious and promising crown. However, my father threw that away like a rag and returned to his hometown, gathering children from the neighborhood to teach them Hangul. Young men from the village and occasionally strangers from other places frequented my father's study room. Then one day, the Japanese police came. My father was kicked like a dog by them, bloodied all over, bleeding as he was dragged away with handcuffs on his wrists. In front of my mother, me, and the villagers, he was beaten like a dog led to slaughter. I couldn't even get close to my mother; I was just trembling in fear among the neighborhood kids. I couldn't even cry. I was five years old then." His gaze gradually became distant, as if looking far away. In the cafe, apart from them, only a few students sat silently, absorbed in the music.

Mendelssohn's soul, poignant and sweet, lingered in the air. Darkness began to envelop the evening outside. The towering poplar branches outside the window merged with the fluorescent light escaping through the glass and the twilight, becoming faintly blurred.

The houses, half-hidden in the forest, were submerged into ashiness. It was a time when nothing revealed its true form, the shortest yet warmest moment of the day. Ji-ae cherished such times, viewing them as periods of rest when nature subdued human pain and desire, comforting the wounded spirits of mankind. She wished these moments could also soothe his dark memories...

"After that, my father did not return home for a long time. However, when he finally did, I could no longer recognize him. He had been severely tortured by them. Upon returning, he almost completely abstained from food and was unable to stand. He couldn't even make it to the bathroom, and my mother had to care for him. At that time, I was in my third year of school. Father lived like that for perhaps a year. It's astonishing how resilient a human life can be. Despite everything, he somehow retained his strength, always cursing Japan. He expressed no desire to die. Instead, he wished to see Japan fall and witness Korea's liberation with his own eyes. Throughout that year, our home was torn apart and bruised by my father's curses and rage, his battle against the death that seemed reserved for him..."

"...However, my father deeply longed for..."

My father passed away without witnessing the liberation of our homeland or the downfall of Japan. His death was tragically harrowing. Bedridden all day, his body decayed, yet his mind remained sharp. My grandmother tried to send me outside to spare me from seeing it, but my grandfather insisted on having me sit on his lap to witness the end. I felt as though my entire body would freeze in terror. With his eyes bloodshot, my father screamed one last time at my grandfather, "Father, I do not wish to die. I must live." Those were his final words."

Silence ensued. Tchaikovsky, Brahms, and Mendelssohn had long vacated the premises. The owner, sitting idly behind the counter, silently urged us to leave for the night. "Let's go. I apologize for monopolizing your valuable time with my story," he said as he stood up. "No, please don't say that!" Tears welled up in my eyes; I turned my head away, not wanting him to see. The countless hours without him, his presence never leaving me for a moment, Ji-ae looked at him with the pain of knowing she could no longer meet him. In his gaze, an unspoken word was blossoming: love. For them, love was still an ambiguous term, the desperation to grasp its meaning was just as painful.

At the Year-End Party

From the onset, there was a scorching sensation on her lips. A few days had elapsed since Christmas. "Why does your face look like that? You almost seem lovesick," Miyoung exclaimed with an air of exaggeration. Ji-ae rolled her eyes in response. "I couldn't sleep last night, that's all." "Don't you have the year-end party tonight?" "I do, but I'm not sure. If you were going..." "Why would I? It's not like I'm an alumnus." "I just don't want to go alone." "Really? Then shall we go? Maybe I'll snag a boyfriend!" chuckled Miyoung. That evening, as they took Shim's car to the designated meeting place...

The parking space at the venue was already hard to find. "It seems everyone makes time for the reunion, no matter how busy they are." "You said it's your first time attending, right?" "Yes, it's the first time we've gathered on such a grand scale. Oh, look, there's a friend. Hey! The doctor graces us with his presence." Shim waved his hand excitedly. A middle-aged gentleman with a neat appearance, accompanied by a woman in a glamorous evening dress and a mink shawl, came into view. "Hey, this is my wife. Say hello." "Ah, the lady of the house! I apologize for my delayed greeting. How could you keep such a beauty hidden?" Shim playfully tapped his shoulder. "I've heard a lot about you." She stood by her husband with a somewhat haughty and provocative pose. "Oh, please, allow me to introduce you. This is Dr. Kim, and over there is Ji-ae. My wife couldn't make it due to our child being unwell." "Is that so? That's unfortunate. I had been looking forward to meeting her... Pleased to meet you." Dr. Oh extended his hand to greet the women. The conference hall, located on a hill and spanned three floors, twinkled with dazzling lights. Ji-ae felt her heart fluttering for no reason. A cocktail party was in full swing. Being her first time at such an event, she felt out of place.

As the cocktail hour ended and people began to gather in the main conference hall, Miyoung was left talking with Dr. Oh while Ji-ae stepped away to dispose of her empty plate.

At that moment, Ji-ae felt a piercing gaze directed at her and lifted her head. She was breathless. Ah, it was Hyun. Hyun was definitely there. Standing amidst the crowd, rooted to the spot, his eyes fixed on her. In the enveloping darkness, a solitary light flashed, swirling into oblivion, casting a beacon of chaos. There he stood, as if twenty years were merely a piece of paper, folded and tossed into the void. She couldn't move. If this was a dream, or even if it wasn't...

In his eyes lay twenty years of surprise and shock, seeming to speak volumes. They conveyed longing, an assurance of remembrance, inquiries about her well-being and happiness, and whether the promise they made to each other upon parting—to find happiness—had been kept. These questions simmered between them. A smile, more refined, deeper, and with a clearer intention, flickered at the corners of his mouth, as fragile as leaves rustling in the autumn breeze. The fluorescent light carried countless unspoken words to Ji-ae, delving into her eyes...

Sparks flew in her heart. Ah, twenty years, our twenty years! He approached her. He took her hand. It was warm. For a while, they stood as still as statues. Then, he opened his mouth to speak.

His voice trembled out, dull as if burdened with a severe illness. "What brings you here?" Ji-ae, with her hand clasped in his, felt a dizzying sensation as if her body was spinning. "Hey, what are you doing here? Oh! Teacher, you're here? But..."

Just then, Miyoung approached, eyes wide, alternately examining the two of them. "Ah, Miyoung, hello," he said, releasing Ji-ae's hand, sounding flustered. Miyoung walked over to Ji-ae and asked, "Hey, are you feeling alright? You've been off since this morning." "No, I'm fine. Just a bit of a headache. I'd like to sit down." "Yes, that might be best." Miyoung pulled up a chair for Ji-ae to sit. "Well, I should get going..." Hyun glanced back at Ji-ae and Miyoung before following the crowd.

"You're acting strangely. And so is Jin." Ji-ae leaned on the table, propping her arms up to cradle her head. A vast white wall seemed to flutter away in the wind. Her strength ebbed away. So, this can happen in the world too. Miyoung didn't pry any further. Ji-ae stood up. "I'm okay now."

"I'm sorry." "Let's head to the restroom." "Okay." Ji-ae followed Miyoung to the restroom. "My goodness, how long has it been?" "Indeed, how long?" "I'd say, about twelve years?" Two women in glamorous evening attire hugged each other, chatting away like children. The sound of "The East Sea and Mount Baekdu" resonated powerfully to the accompaniment of a grand instrumental, as if buildings themselves might take off with the booming chorus. This was followed by the singing of the school anthem, lighting the torch of truth atop Mount Gwanak... The scent of lilac flowers wafted through. The corners of the schoolyard where winds once swept piles of fallen leaves, and there was Hyun. "MJi-ae, have you ever seen death?" Ah, had he now overcome that death? How had he dealt with the apparitions that his father's death had brought him? They found their designated seats. It seemed they were the only pair not coupled by gender at the gathering. "May I sit here?" A deep, masculine voice sounded right by her ear. It was Shim Min-guk. "Ah, Shim. Of course. We wondered where you had vanished to." Miyoung remained her usual self.

"Ha, but where did that friend go?" Shim half-rose, looking around as if searching for someone. "Did you meet Jin Hyun? Ji-ae, I saw him briefly earlier, but where did he go?" "Yes, just for a moment." "Shim, you know Dr. Jin too?" Miyoung glanced at Ji-ae before turning to Shim. "Indeed, we were in the same department, same batch. But how do you know Dr. Kim?" "We met at a gathering, and afterwards, he invited me several times to discuss issues related to youth." "Youth issues?" Shim raised his eyebrows. "Ah, it's a bit difficult to talk about. It's Dr. Jin's privacy, after all." Miyoung chuckled awkwardly. "Ah, that friend is quite unique. I thought he just sold coffee, but does he do something else?" Shim added thoughtfully. "Indeed, he's a unique individual. He was once a professor, a war correspondent..." "Really? He sounds like a fascinating person." Perhaps it was the alcohol, but Miyoung's face turned red as she chatted away. Ji-ae simply listened to their conversation. "But why is he still unmarried?

Has he been married before? Divorced? Or perhaps he has a wife in Korea?"

"Ah, take a breath before you speak," Shim teased, causing Miyoung's face to redden even further. "Oh, teacher too..." Ji-ae moistened her lips with a cup filled with ice water. "Jin Hyun has his eccentricities," Shim diverted the conversation from Miyoung's question without directly responding. "He was about to go to Germany for further studies, possibly to become a priest, but at the last moment, he enlisted in the military. After being discharged, he returned to academia, where he was recruited as a lecturer at our university due to his brilliant intellect. While lecturing, he also published articles in journals and was on his way to securing a professorship, but then he abruptly left it all behind for something completely unexpected..."

"What unexpected thing?" Miyoung was fully drawn into his story.

"Back then, the Vietnam War was at its height, and the fervor for it was intense here. He came to me, dressed in military uniform, saying he was leaving to become a war correspondent the next day and wanted to see me one last time. I felt like I had been hit on the head about ten times. 'Hey, man. Are you insane?' But he just laughed it off. After that, there was no word from him, but a year ago, I walked into a coffee shop on 7th Avenue, No. 32, and there he was, wearing an apron. I was absolutely flabbergasted." After sharing this, perhaps because of the alcohol, he abruptly stopped talking and closed his mouth tight.

"Indeed, that's quite a story!" Miyoung spoke in a dreamy tone, as if lost in thought. "Oh, look who has decided to show up now," she remarked as Hyun navigated between the tables towards their seats. Ji-ae's face flushed instantly, feeling as though all strength had drained from her body. "Even a tiger..." Shim teased, giving Hyun a playful tap on the shoulder as he sat down beside them. "Why lag behind the topic? Sorry about that. I was greeting a senior, so..." Hyun alternated glances between Miyoung and Ji-ae, offering a smile and an apology. "Don't worry, we were just enjoying some interesting stories. Right, Ji-ae?" Miyoung sought Ji-ae's agreement. "Yes." Ji-ae produced a smile as ethereal as mist. "This man is something else. To see him so popular among the ladies," Shim chuckled heartily. Hyun offered a brief smile, then let his gaze drift aimlessly to a vase on the table. Ji-ae felt her mouth go dry. What could he be thinking about, standing before me after twenty years? Ji-ae chastised herself, trying hard to act nonchalantly. The atmosphere at the table momentarily turned solemn.

"Let's raise our glasses. To our gathering and friendship," Shim, holding up his half-finished drink, initiated a toast. 'Our meeting...' Ji-ae silently echoed the sentiment, glancing at Hyun. He, too, caught her eye in that moment. A light was ignited. The flame seemed to swiftly invade every corner of her being, leaving behind a trail of exquisite pain as it flickered. "To our meeting and friendship," Miyoung echoed Shim, lifting her glass high. Then, the clinking sound of four glasses meeting resonated before they were set down again. Ji-ae brought her glass of orange juice to her lips.

"So, how have you been lately? Not a word from you, this friend here has been waiting for me to reach out. All the way to New York, to see an old friend," Hyun spoke, hinting at a mix of jest and earnestness. Soon after, food arrived, and the evening progressed with introductions from the host, welcoming words from the alumni association president, and then various performances by departmental groups commenced. "You've really outdone yourself recently. We plan to have more gatherings like this in the future. We'll be needing Miyoung's assistance even more," Hyun remarked, directing his words toward Miyoung. "Of course, anytime," she responded eagerly. "Thank you."

Hyun's earnest voice was heard, "Then, I'll return to my seat." He stood up and went back to his designated seat. Ji-ae was thankful for the space he left; it allowed her a moment of respite.

"That friend, as odd as his actions may sometimes be, as I said earlier, is extraordinary. I hold him in high regard. There are inexplicable aspects to him, but his actions are decisively right or wrong... And it's not that he's unkind; he's genuinely a great guy."

"It seems you're quite the fan of Dr. Jin. I'm getting jealous here," Miyoung joked, her spirits higher than usual.

"As I mentioned earlier, when I unexpectedly ran into him wearing an apron, I really thought I was seeing things. I was happy to see him, yet anger welled up inside me without reason. So I blurted out, 'Hey, what are you doing? Don't you have better things to do than to come here and do this?' But he just gave me this big grin, as if he was meeting an old friend after just having seen them the day before. He seemed so at ease. He's changed a lot."

"In what way?"

"It's just... I felt a completely different vibe from him than before he left for Vietnam." The two women urged him to elaborate.

"Well, it's hard to say exactly... It's something I hadn't felt before," he trailed off, hinting at a profound transformation in Hyun that words could scarcely capture.

"Is it another side of him, or perhaps a new aspect? It's hard to pinpoint, but there's an ambiance about him that I hadn't felt before, with none of the darkness that used to be there."

"It sounds like you're narrating a detective novel. Isn't it natural for Dr. Jin to seem like a different person? He was once a respected professor, and now in New York, he's an apron-wearing coffee shop owner. Plus, a lot of time has passed," Miyoung clarified.

"No, it's not that. I don't judge a person by their appearance," he insisted.

"Forgive me, then. What do you mean exactly when you say he's changed?"

"Well, how should I put it? It seems like a personal transformation. It's as if all the knots that were tightly bound have come undone, and there's this relaxed aura about him now. As if he's escaped from some prison of consciousness he was fatefully trapped in... Ah, let's drop it," he gestured dismissively.

"Maybe Dr. Jin became a philosopher of sorts, confronting death in Vietnam, undergoing the ultimate life-altering experience, and that's why..."

"Miyoung makes it sound straightforward, but there's something deeper, something indescribable I sensed. We've been friends for a long time."

"Ji-ae, why are you just listening? You look like you're lost in a dream."

As the band started playing, people began to rise and pair off to dance. Shim took Miyoung out to the dance floor. Ji-ae, claiming a headache, remained seated, simply watching them. The thought that he had changed kept circling in her mind. The man who left for Vietnam and the man in the apron at the coffee shop were not the same... Shim's words echoed in her thoughts. Miyoung's question, "Why is he alone?" shimmered amidst the kaleidoscopic neon lights, making the dancing couples seem like seaweed swaying in water. Ji-ae lifted her gaze to search for the table where Hyun had disappeared. He was still there, his back turned, engaged in a serious conversation with another man. A sense of solemnity hovered around his broad shoulders. As the music ended and people returned to their seats, Miyoung, flushed from the dance, said, "Hey, Ji-ae. Shim leads well. You should try dancing too." "Give it a try," Shim also encouraged her. When the music shifted to a blues track, Shim approached Ji-ae. Unable to refuse any longer, she stood up. "Ji-ae, you dance quite well. Where did you learn?" Shim maintained a respectful distance as they danced. "It's necessary; I'm not very good. It's because you lead well..." "But you do dance well."

Upon returning to their seats, Miyoung teased Ji-ae. She turned her head towards where Hyun was sitting. He was still engrossed in conversation, unchanged from before. "Excuse me for a moment," Shim excused himself from the table. With Shim gone, Miyoung leaned in, her tone playful yet probing, "Ji-ae, was there something between you and Hyun?" "No, we just used to attend the same gatherings back in the day. That's all," Ji-ae replied. "But why were you like that earlier? You're acting strange. It's definitely not normal. You've been odd all evening. Are you playing coy?" Miyoung playfully pinched the back of Ji-ae's hand. "Think what you want." "Would you like to dance?" Dr. Oh had approached their table at some point, looking alternately at Ji-ae and Miyoung as he asked. "Miyoung, why don't you dance? Sorry, I'm not much of a dancer." Miyoung rolled her eyes at Ji-ae before standing up. Dr. Oh took the seat across from

Ji-ae. "It's like a dream," he said. "I was truly surprised earlier. It was unbelievable to see Ji-ae suddenly appearing before me."

His gaze carried a weight. "...Me too." It was dizzying, having him sit before her felt like a dream. "I understand. You don't need to say it," his voice was faint, like letters not fully erased by a rubber. Silence lingered. For a moment, their eyes deeply intertwined. His face seemed to fade into a mist. The meeting was overwhelming. "Ji-ae, you haven't changed at all." "Nor have you, Hyun." "What? I've changed a lot. And now I'm old," Hyun said with a faint smile. "How can you say that!" "Meeting Ji-ae like this makes me suddenly feel melancholic. Perhaps it's the sorrow of realizing how much time has passed. I'm not even sure of myself anymore." A heavy thud resounded in her heart. Ah, he too had been measuring the years. In his face, now devoid of its former luster, she saw the elapsed time. The face that once brimmed with youth now bore the subtle pain of fine lines beneath the eyes. "You must be married by now." "Yes."

A fleeting shadow of wrinkles appeared on his face. "Ah, I see. That's how it should be." He lightly punched the air with his right fist, nodding his head in rhythm as if keeping time with his taps. "Do you have children?" "One, just one." "They must have grown a lot." "And you, Hyun?" "Me? My story? Let's save that for another time," his response was evasive. "I should be going then." He bowed his head to Ji-ae as if he had urgent matters to attend to, then made his way to the exit. Why would he leave like that? She felt his departure was profoundly lonely, stirring a surge of compassion within her. At that moment, memories of her late mother surfaced. After a period of silence following the year-end party, Miyoung called out of the blue. "There's a gathering for Hyun tonight. I'll stop by after work. Let's go together." Miyoung was in a hurry. "Wait! I won't go. You go on without me."

"Why? Are you feeling unwell? You've got nothing else planned for the evening."

"Yeah, I'm just tired. Sorry." I can't possibly go. How would I fit in with Miyoung and those young people? Better not to go at all.

"Well, can't be helped then. I'll call you after I get back," Miyoung ended the call.

46

The next day, Miyoung found Ji-ae during lunchtime. Reluctantly, Ji-ae agreed to join her for lunch at the cafeteria, unable to find an excuse to decline.

"It's strange, you know. You and Hyun seem to be suffering from the same ailment. The look on Hyun's face last night wasn't normal," Miyoung's gaze was different from usual as she sneakily observed Ji-ae's reaction.

"So now you're a psychiatrist, reading minds too?"

"Right, you caught me. I'm a mirror of the mind. Anyone who reflects in my mirror can't hide their true feelings. Ji-ae, tell me. Are you in love with Hyun? How long has this been going on? Let's clear the air."

"Sorry, I can't lie to you. It's been a long time. Since our school days."

"Ah, I see." Miyoung's gaze darkened as she stared intently at Ji-ae. "And this meeting was the first time in how many years?"

"20 years."

"No, 20 years, that's too long," sympathy pooled in Miyoung's eyes, as if touched by the chill of winter rain. "All this time, not knowing if the other was alive or dead."

"Yes."

"It's quite a tragic tale."

Ji-ae found herself speechless.

"So that's why he hasn't married till now. And I was unaware..."

"It's not certain. He's always been hard to read."

"There must be a reason he hasn't married till now, right?"

"We weren't like that."

"Then?"

"I don't know," Ji-ae said forcefully, turning her head away.

"Why? If both of you wanted to..."

"We were told,"

"Told? Love isn't something you hear; it's forceful. Don't act like the old generation. If you want to see someone, just meet them, right?"

"I don't understand those things."

"You're being foolish. Your husband is out there living his life in Korea."

Ji-ae's face turned red as she looked at Miyoung. Do I not also long for him? But how can I become a perpetrator of love's violence if he does not reach out to me? "Let's drop this topic, shall we?"

"So, it's okay if I steal Hyun away? Not that it's possible, since he seems completely indifferent," Miyoung said, looking dejected.

Observing Miyoung's reaction, Ji-ae thought, 'Ah, to what extent does Miyoung fancy Hyun?'

"But you seem to have had your share of love woes. To still be single, was it because you loved someone so much you could die?" Miyoung's face quickly darkened, and it was as if rain began to fall.

"I once had feelings for my cousin, my mother's nephew. After graduating from college, he committed suicide out of pessimism. He could have been a great scholar in German literature."

"That's tragic. I had no idea, dredging up old wounds like that."

"It's not like that. It's always there, now part of who I am, embedded in my cells. But somehow, I feel he might have done it because of me. He was such a precious person." Miyoung's gaze dimmed, looking far away. Shadows fell over her pale, round face as rain seemed to seep from a distance.

"…"

"Actually, I like Hyun too. I met him at a gathering two years ago, and the moment I saw him, my heart just sank. Later, I understood why. He was exactly like my cousin."

"Ah, why does life have to be so painful?"

"If it weren't for the pain, the world might just burst at its sealmagine the chaos if everyone started inventing their own elixir of life, huh!"

"Miyoung, you're amazing. I completely give up to you."

"Thanks, let's eat this and become strong warriors." Miyoung forcefully stabbed her fork into the spaghetti, scooping up a generous amount and munching on it exaggeratedly.

"But Ji-ae, don't be like that. When it's time to love, you should love. After death, the emptiness is indescribable. Of course, we were in a relationship where love wasn't possible, but there's a time to hate and a time to love, they said. Then you die, and just like that, it all ends."

"Who said that? You're really a mess."

"So what? I speak from what I feel."

"How can you live like that?" Ji-ae looked at Miyoung anew.

"I have my job. Patients come with their pain, opening up their hearts to

"When they entrust me with their problems, I completely forget about my own existence. At the end of the day, I'm thankful for the day that's ended, recalling the faces of my patients one by one as I drift into sleep from exhaustion. That's my life. I don't have a white, black, or yellow 'baby.' In the face of pain, all human faces are of one color; pain unifies everyone into a single hue, and so does hope."

"..."

"Ji-ae, longing is the same."

Tears welled up in Miyoung's eyes. She seemed completely drenched, a side of her friend Ji-ae had never seen. Miyoung, always playful and cheerful, carried such wounds. In her heart, Ji-ae reached out and grasped her friend's wrist.

"I'm pathetic, aren't I?"

"No, I'm thankful and proud of you."

"Thank you."

They stood up. As they were leaving the cafeteria, they bumped into Hong, the office manager, coming in.

The Wandering Theater

"I'm a step late, it seems." "As always, Hong is one step behind," Miyoung retorted sharply. "Oh, why do you say that? Dr. Kim seems quite upset today." "Not at all. I'm one hundred percent in a good mood," Miyoung flashed a grin, showing her thumb up before quickly heading out the door. "Ji-ae, let's have dinner together sometime." He tried to catch up to Ji-ae, who was following Miyoung. "I wonder if that's necessary." "Does there need to be a necessity? It's just dinner. I'll come by in the evening." Ji-ae didn't respond further and quickly moved away from him. "Be careful with that man. It's suspicious, him being here all by himself without his family."

A few days ago, Miyoung's words came back to her. As Ji-ae was preparing to leave work in the evening, Hong, the office manager, entered. "Ah, you're still here," he said, catching Ji-ae off guard. "You haven't forgotten our dinner appointment, have you?" "I didn't make any promise, though." "Don't say that. Let's go out. I happen to have two tickets. Someone is performing a monologue called The Wandering Theater. Let's have dinner and then go there." He was persistent. Ji-ae was intrigued more by the mention of The Wandering Theater than the dinner with him. Living in America, she always felt a hunger for anything Korean. She decided to accompany him.

After a simple meal, they arrived to find the play had already begun. There was no elaborate stage setup, just a middle-aged man, comically draped in an ill-fitting, shabby suit, passionately addressing the audience seated in a circle around him.

"...The sorrow and rage of losing our country during the Japanese occupation, and our hopes for liberation, gave birth to The Wandering Theater. Now, everyone, there are no separate actors or audience here; we are all performers in this traveling theater."

His voice, rising dramatically at the end of each sentence, boiled with intensity.

"Our ancestors were a nomadic people, originating from the Mongolian region, moving southward in search of dreams until they could go no further, stopped by the sea, and thus established a nation at the edge of the continent. A people in white, who knew not of harming others, yet for 36 years, fell under the violence of Japanese rule, with peasants being stripped of their ancestral lands and intellectuals of their spiritual fields, either exiled or leaving without politics. And then, what about the Korean War? Fleeing the red menace from the North, from Seoul, the southern harbors were overwhelmed by the tragedy of a national conflict. Now, what has driven you to move to this farthest and most foreign land?"

His voice, both exaggerated and stirring, flowed smoothly.

"Tonight, however, I want to share a piece of our proud history, about our compatriots who went to Sakhalin during the Japanese occupation. In 1923, Russia deported our people from their settlements to the vast plains of Central Asia. They were driven into the heart of Central Asia, a death field frozen solid in the bitter winter. But, ah, when they opened the doors of the train at their destination, a settlement without homes or temples, do you know what they found? My dear compatriots, do not be shocked. What they saw, gathered in a circle, holding hands in death, were our people, all dead."

The theater fell into a somber silence. His husky voice.

Without even taking a sip of water, he continued, "But do not be alarmed. On the outermost part were the elderly, then the middle-aged, holding shoulders, forming a circle, frozen in death. And please, do not be shocked, dear compatriots, but within the embrace of these deceased middle-aged people, the young ones were still alive." He added a poignant emphasis at the end of his speech.

"Do you even realize that these are the forebears of our proud Koryo-saram, the descendants of our nation who make us proud today? What more explanation is needed?"

Suddenly, his pace quickened. "We must not forget. The perseverance our nation possesses, the spirit of collectively moving forward with dreams in our hearts, and the broad-mindedness to share whatever little we have, like sharing rice cakes with the entire neighborhood whenever there is a birthday at one house or a special occasion. And remember, the spirit of coming together in times of crisis. Everyone, everyone! These are the things we must never forget, no matter how unstable, difficult, or challenging our reality becomes. And the haste, haste for good things...?"

A giggle burst from the audience at this point.

"Of course, 'haste, haste' isn't always good. It's when we rush and end up forgetting the good, like manners, for instance. Or, let's say, on the rare occasion a couple goes out..."

"The rush of the women urged by their husbands to hurry up, do you know where this 'hurry, hurry' originates? Isn't it from our nation's tragic and painful history of losing our homeland and being driven from place to place? The journey is long, and as the sun begins to set in the west... But did you know this became the fertilizer that stirred a miraculous wind across our land of three thousand ri? The problem is our propensity to forget the past too easily, to forget the paths our ancestors have walked. Above all, how proud our history is, how Baekje was taken, but its people, taken wholesale to Japan, laid the foundations for today's Japanese culture through their contributions to the royal household, pottery, and more...

Look, Japan keeps its mouth tightly shut. You might say, 'So what? It's all in the past...' But though time passes, the substance within it does not disappear. We must take this substance as our nourishment for today. What I want to say this evening is that we should live today with pride in ourselves. There's something else I want to mention, another virtue of ours. Our nation's ancestors were known for their spirit of sacrifice, even to the extent of sacrificing themselves for what is right. The wise principle of 'Hongik Ingan,' benefiting all mankind, is our unique traditional culture. And there's also the 'respect for heaven and love for people,' once proudly displayed on our homes' large wooden floors, a spirit that is, sadly, fading away."

The actor's voice resonated deeply, touching on the enduring values and sacrifices of the Korean people, a call to remember and honor their rich cultural heritage and the spirit of 'Hongik Ingan' that has historically defined them.

"You must not forget the foundation of our spirit, even here in this distant land of America." After taking a sip of water from the glass on the table, he scanned the audience, a quiet earnestness writhing within him. Under the dim red lights, his sweat-soaked face shone, his eyes burning with the intensity of a sunbeam in the deep, compassionate heart.

'What makes him so desperately passionate?' As Ji-ae watched, memories of her father, grandfather, mother, an elderly man she met on the plane to America, and the sturdy zelkova tree at the entrance of her hometown village surfaced. She noticed a few foreigners among the audience as well. He pulled a handkerchief from his pocket to wipe his lips, then continued speaking. Ji-ae thought the handkerchief seemed exceptionally white.

"Our nation has always been one to pursue dreams, not merely because our reality has been harsh. Even when we are away from our homeland, it lives within our hearts, always breathing within us. In ancient times, in the land of eternal morning that shone on Mount Taebaek, our ancestors captured fire from the heavens to dream and nurture our spirit. My beloved brothers and sisters, do you know this truth?"

To enhance the dramatic delivery and content of his monologue, the sound of drums and a janggu emanated from behind a screen set up on stage, sometimes like a gentle breeze among flowers, at other times like heavy raindrops falling on rocks, resonating loudly.

Ji-ae sat immersed in the flood of his words, momentarily forgetting to speak, and along with the other audience members, she sent a smile filled with deep respect to Han Dong-sik, the monologue actor. "Tonight, he spoke of our nation as one of perseverance and tears, and how our 'hurry, hurry' spirit will surely propel us onto the world stage... What do you think, Ji-ae?" The office manager asked as he drove her home. Ji-ae remained silent, listening to him, overwhelmed by the emotions stirred by the performance.

However, Ji-ae felt uneasy. The issues plaguing the youth reported in the homeland's newspapers. And not just that. The roots of corruption appearing across politics, economy, education, and society at large. Where do these roots begin? With economic revival, how do we address the rampant individualism and greed, and where is the path for a society where ethics and morals don't grow alongside economic development, and what truly constitutes progress? Ji-ae feared these questions.

"Let's take a break," the office manager suddenly stopped the car next to a cemetery. It was as silent as death.

"It's late," Ji-ae asserted with force in her voice, sensing a threat. However, ignoring her words, he turned off the car's ignition and suddenly wrapped his arm around her shoulder in a tight embrace. "Oh no, this shouldn't happen," Ji-ae struggled to wriggle out of his grasp, using all her strength to escape. But he persisted stubbornly. His sticky lips forcefully covered hers. With one arm, he held her shoulder, and with the other, he reached under her skirt, easily grasping her bare skin, as she wasn't wearing stockings. Feeling the imminent danger, Ji-ae bit his lips in desperation. "Ouch, what are you doing!" he recoiled and sat back. "I'm sorry. But, how could you!" "I didn't know Miss Ji-ae was so strong," he taunted with a smug red face. "Look at that grave. In their orderly and tranquil dwelling," "I'm sorry!" The office manager remained silent until they reached home, emanating a complex odor of humiliation and degradation.

The Early Days of Immigration

In the heart of New York, on Broadway, stood a restaurant uniquely owned by a Korean. The place was already bustling with people leaving work and those meeting for business purposes. Ji-ae, feeling her heart flutter to the sound of Korean pop music she hadn't heard in a long time, entered the restaurant. Upon seeing them, Hyun, who had been waiting, promptly stood up. "Hello," Ji-ae felt her heart flutter again as she took a seat next to Mi-young. "It's been quite some time," Hyun said with a smile, looking back and forth between the two women. His boyish grin was as charming as ever. "Dr. Jin, I'm sorry for insisting you come despite your busy schedule." "Not at all. It's a great honor," Ji-ae responded, feeling a sense of comfort in his voice. "Actually, I've been wanting to invite you both out for a while."

"I wouldn't say it's a reason for despair. Nowadays, various organizations are vocal about youth issues and are passionate about programs designed for them. It's as if necessity has started to open doors," he observed. "I hope these programs truly serve the youth and address their problems effectively. Children are being unjustly sacrificed due to parental incompetence and indifference, language barriers, and family breakdowns. Time is of the essence. They are carelessly throwing away precious moments as if discarding them into a trash bin. It's not that we are too greedy," Mi-young looked intently at him. "What do you think, Ji-ae?"

"Well, your conversation is so earnest that it brings to light a regret I've often felt. Coming to the land of opportunity, the United States, and focusing solely on earning money, working like bees, only to miss out on something far more important seems all too common. In a sense, here, where you are rewarded fairly for your work, you don't want to spend that golden time on anything else. And there seems to be a tendency to postpone things that appear less important, adopting a 'wait-a-little-longer' attitude towards our children. It's a somewhat complacent way of thinking. But I believe that's not the right approach," Ji-ae shared her reflections, which were often triggered by the societal issues section in local daily newspapers concerning youth delinquency. "Exactly! Well pointed out. But it's that 'less important' thing that is the problem."

It is unfortunate to let your guard down on things that are never so. There is no time for young people. Education for them doesn't wait. Not knowing the heat when the fire falls on your feet breeds unhappiness." "That's true." "Parents called by the police sometimes threaten their children while being angry, and some parents shed tears and try to persuade them. But what's worse is the kids who don't go to school with the money their divorced fathers send, causing trouble on the streets and getting caught." Ji-ae thought of Mrs. Kim, a Korean immigrant woman who had visited her office a while ago, as she listened to his story. The woman with a face she had met several times in the hospital asked Ji-ae hesitantly if she had time from the beginning. "It's okay. I have plenty of time, so don't worry and talk." Ji-ae lied to calm her mind while organizing the piled-up documents. "Has the child recovered a lot now?" "Yes, she came all the way to the U.S. and almost made her child a fool. Is it reasonable to leave a child alone at home and go out?" Resentment echoed in the woman's voice.

"If you don't want to work, you should take care of your child. I have nothing to be ashamed of now. At first, I tried to live somehow, but then I started gambling, thinking it was easy to make a fortune. Now, all I care about is taking my hard-earned money. What should I do?" The woman, who looked like she was in her early thirties without makeup, looked at Ji-ae with a rough face. There was nothing to say. What can I say in this situation? She said she wanted a divorce, but her husband wouldn't allow it. She said she left her seven-year-old child alone at home, and the child got hurt while playing around. She kept saying it was a relief to quit. She lied to the doctor that they were playing together in the park and the child got hurt by accident.

Ji-ae felt distant from her. In such cases, what I can do is nothing, what I can say, 'It'll be okay, it'll get better soon,' is how irresponsible those words are. People tend to avoid pain, considering it disgusting, but this woman is sitting in the midst of it, chewing on the test and pain her husband gives her bit by bit, as if it were part of her life. "How did you come to the U.S.?" "I came five years ago at the invitation of my sister. She's a nurse." "I see."

"So, it seems he ended up wandering the streets because there wasn't a sturdy pillar holding onto his family." Mi-young's harsh voice summoned Ji-ae from her thoughts. "You could say that. Sang-ho came when he was in the third grade of middle school, so if he had studied hard for a year or two to improve his language skills, today wouldn't be like this. It's not like just going to school improves your English, and he was naturally ostracized at school and the same at home. So he easily found friends in a similar situation as himself. In other words, his unhappiness started from seeking understanding and comfort outside that he didn't get at home and school." Ji-ae, listening to Hyun's words, suddenly wondered why he was burying himself so deeply in the affairs of teenagers. He ran a small coffee shop, yet he didn't hold a position on any of those numerous boards of directors, nor did he involve himself in those many gatherings, quietly walking a lonely path as if it were part of his life. Whose identity is that person, the one who befriends troubled teenagers? At that moment, a rough but dignified voice came from the seat next to where they were sitting. "Why aren't you speaking? How many times did your father tell you? You must speak Korean to your grandparents, didn't your father say that?"

"Hey, stop it. Let the kid eat." "No, Mom. We have to fix it from the beginning. Son, speak up. Grandpa, please give me water," what's 'Give me water'? Son." They all turned their eyes towards the boy. A boy of about six or seven between grandparents and parents, with swollen cheeks and bowed head. Even at a glance, it was clear that the child's pride was severely hurt. With his jaws clenched, he seemed absolutely unwilling to correct what he said. "Get up! Stand over there with your hands up," the father gestured, and the boy stood up hesitantly, tears streaming down his face. Ji-ae sighed inwardly, then glanced at Hyun. His dark gaze met Ji-ae's briefly before quickly sliding away. "He's too much. Education has its time and place." Mi-young clicked her tongue as if she were sure. He glanced at the two women alternately, indicating his intention to leave. They stood up, casting their gaze toward the boy. The boy stopped crying and moved his toes, drawing a small circle on the floor where his tears had fallen. Ah, that boy is growing up like that.

America, Wonders

After meeting Hyun and having dinner together, summer passed. In October, on a clear autumn day, Ji-ae received a call from Haekyung. Haekyung was Ji-ae's only close college friend who stayed near Seoul. She called to have lunch together on the weekend. "Why don't you ever call? Are you really living on the moon or something?" Haekyung scolded as soon as Ji-ae appeared at the agreed place. "Sorry. I've been busy." "Ah, cut it out. What are you busy with? Living alone. Are you making a fortune in your youth business?" "This one talks too much!" Ji-ae chuckled. "Anyway, it's good to see you."

Haekyung looked at Ji-ae anew as she spoke. "I haven't heard from you since we met at the church last time, so today I left my family at home to catch up with you." "Is your family doing well?" "Our little ones at home are all doing well, and the big boss is fine too." Pride and warm breeze emanated from her face. "But why does your face look like that? You don't look good. Do you even have any contact with your husband?" "No, you know too." "What kind of answer is that?" "But how about your husband?" Ji-ae quickly changed the subject. "He's the same. Orders flooded in after promoting the new wig products, and he's swamped. He hasn't even come home. Heheh. But how's your son?" "He's good. His girlfriend called again last night. She's an American kid studying in the same department. But she's really nice." "Oh, has it come to that already?" Ji-ae imagined what her old friend's happy family life might be like. It was the day they happened to meet at church. After nearly twenty years of not seeing each other, they hugged each other, shedding tears while laughing as they walked together, and her husband invited Ji-ae to their home. "Come on. Can we just let an old friend we met after so long go like this?"

He gently pulled the hesitating Ji-ae. "We're still living like this without a home." Although it hadn't been long since he started a small business opening several wig shops near Washington Square, his confidence overflowed due to curiosity about Korean products or perhaps because of the rush of orders. Ji-ae carefully looked around their apartment, which was neither flashy nor shabby, but well organized with modest decorations and furniture. "If we can get a loan from the bank, we can afford a small house. But Junghui can't forget this place like an old lover." "Well, who doesn't resist moving?" He chuckled playfully. Listening to their affectionate and genuine conversation, Ji-ae unintentionally thought of her husband. That's what a real home looks like. Two people becoming one after leaving their parents... "Let's have lunch here and then go out to Washington Square. You won't be bored there." Looking at Haekyung, who seemed even livelier than in her school days, Ji-ae wondered what had made her like that. Seeing her old friend so subtly happy, Ji-ae couldn't shake off the sadness of being a loser in life. Who said, 'Marriage is a gamble.'

Then maybe we started off on the wrong foot? You can't expect good results from a bad hand. The harsh reality of giving and receiving as much as you can from each other. But what if we can't share? If we reject each other like ice floes floating in the Arctic Ocean, or if one side triggers a rejection response? Which side are we on? No, are we both? Ji-ae bit back a sigh. "Don't you get bored staying at home all day?" Ji-ae said, pondering. "What boredom? I'm actually busy these days. I started working." "Oh, really? Where?" "From about a month ago, I can go out a few days a week to work in a cosmetics store. How could a homemaker like me have a sharp nose? But I can't go to my husband's store, he's against it. That's the only thing I can't do. Hehe!" She chuckled happily as she put extra emphasis on her last words. "I understand him. Wouldn't anyone get tired even if they're on good terms? Imagine staring at the same face for twenty-four hours a day. In fact, such a thing happened recently. At first, the couple got along well, then they started arguing, and eventually, they divorced. Such a thing happened close to us." "Is that so?" "It was uncomfortable for the first few days, but hey, once I realized work is just the same, I felt revitalized."

"Yeah, you should just do what you like, whether it's at the White House desk or playing horseback." "Yeah, that's right. You have to be able to endure the boredom of being in a house where all the kids have grown up. But you can't just go out and meet friends like in Seoul." "Yeah, you did well." "At first, he was against it, but as the kids grew up, he allowed it when I insisted." "Now your siblings will be fine." Ji-ae recalled the time when Haekyung took care of her siblings without their father. "Yeah, they're all doing well," Haekyung's voice became a mix of pride and relief. "You did well." "Oh, it was nothing. They're smart, that's all." "I've always admired you. I envied you. You had a sense of responsibility and seemed happy with so many siblings." The autumn sun leaned towards one side, reminiscent of the Independence Gate in Seoul's Seodaemun, and the shape of New York's Independence Arch began to emerge in the shade. There is a morning inscription commemorating the 100th anniversary of America's first president, George Washington, who is said to have spoken to soldiers during the War of Independence.

"Let us raise a standard to which the wise and honest can repair. The event is in the hand of God." People gather here and there to see the sights. In a corner of the playground, a young man twirls a cast-iron pot lid, three times the size of his head, on his fingertips without any spectators. In the center of the square, two same-sex partners arm in arm enjoy roller skating and acrobatics. The elderly seemed to be there just to pass the time. They are New Yorkers who have become accustomed to not being interested in other people's affairs. Even if men appear in strange costumes with their arms linked, no one pays any attention. Under the late sunlight, time floats lighter than dust, with freedom and fun. It doesn't bother with nuclear war, the tragedy in Libya, the issue of division in Korea, or Reagan's tax cuts. "This is a no-fly zone, and you can see at a glance how trends and culture are moving here. But no one cares about such things," Haekyung said, looking around at the sun without saying a word, her voice dripping like droplets.

"Well, when I see those people, I feel more sad than amused. Whether it's people making jokes in the crowd, or young people showing off their skills without an audience, they all seem to be trying to escape boredom and despair..............." "No, they're just spending their time and energy idly, without any thought." "Is that so? Haekyung, I'm not sure if what you're saying is right." Just then, a young man played a trumpet, its golden sound sparkling in the sunlight. Toot, toot, to, God Bless America. Waves of golden light flooded in with the clear autumn sunlight. "Hey, are you still writing poetry?" Haekyung looked at Ji-ae anew. "Poetry? My well has dried up now." "Remember the old days? I always read your poetry. Even though it wasn't your major, you were always writing poetry, publishing in the university newspaper and even in magazines. Doesn't that make sense to you? I believe that one day, poetry will pour out of you like a waterfall." "Will it? I don't even know what's what anymore. I think I made a mistake coming to America. If I had stayed in Korea, at least I could have taken care of my mom until now." "Look at those kids!"

Haekyung let out a small sigh. How long had it been flying? Pigeons and seagulls were pecking at the ground beneath their feet. "Even here, seagulls and pigeons mingle well with people without having to go far out to sea... But America is a scary place. Do they look so innocent? But if they have even a slight vested interest, they'll notice you. Koreans don't know them." "They can't help it............. Considering how a country with such a short history has become a leader in global culture, there is an inexplicable power in the depths of American culture." "If you feel that way, it's probably because of the vast land of this country." "Is that so? Anyway, it holds the unique culture of immigration, infused with that power. American multi-culturalism is probably created quietly and subtly. And they have their own order and friendship." "......" "We can't ignore the spirit of benevolence underlying their fundamental spirit." As long as that spirit is alive in any society or country, she thought, she could hear her words in the hospital and happily volunteer for the children. Of course, it wasn't just Julie. Where did the volunteer culture, so prevalent in this country, begin? "Oh, by the way, why didn't you go to

Korea? Where's a good place to live like in Korea? With money, that place is number one in the world."

"No, that's the problem. What comes easily also goes easily because they don't know its value. A society without a culture of sacrifice is dangerous, and I have no confidence... in anything." She thought. If only her mother were still alive....... The regret, like left-over food scraps, of not being able to protect her mother's death, not being able to attend her funeral, still bleeds in her heart. The afternoon sun brought a cool breeze. People were disappearing one by one. Even the so-called actors were gone, and in the empty square, like the final scene of a silent movie, a man in a fur coat appeared. He walked past them with aimless steps, wearing a glossy brown suit that shone with the years and times. He seemed to be going under a tall chestnut tree, but then he looked up at the tree. As if bidding farewell to someone he missed, he soon laid out a fur and lay down neatly, as if performing a religious ritual. And then he closed his eyes. Now call me, I am ready to go... It seemed as if he was singing a comfortable eternal sleep. At the entrance where they came out, a young white Hindu was sitting under a blue sky-colored cloth sprinkled with silver dust. "Are you meditating?" he asked. "Of course."

Haekyung laughed and grabbed Ji-ae's hand casually. "We should go home and make dinner. Our captain and the lieutenants must be hungry." Her friend's exaggerated expression didn't sound disgusting at all. Ji-ae suddenly thought of a ship resting in the harbor. A serene place with gentle waves lapping, that was the true image of a home. Even if storms and hurricanes raged outside, inside there was joy and peace, the essence of a home, home sweet home. It was amazing and sad to think that such a place existed on the streets of New York.

Conflict

The morning light is faintly rising. The chestnut trees standing in the mist-shrouded apartment garden are fully absorbing the chirping of birds in the gray mist. It had been over a month since Ji-ae met Haekyung. In her dreams, she was being pursued by a man. A bundle of inexplicable anger and mountain-like sorrows fills her throat. Why am I trembling like this? Is my source and goal of pain simply blaming Hyun, that person? Is it an effort to possess him just for the sake of his existence in New York? No, it's probably not just that. Ji-ae, spinning in circles of thoughts, suddenly felt like she was playing a prank on herself. Oh God, how far will I go? How far will I thoroughly endure pain and reach the depths of despair? Hyun said that God is beyond despair, that God gives peace and rest.

Hyun had said that God gives peace and rest. It felt like his quiet yet fervent voice from the distant past, twenty years ago, was echoing. His facial contours were creased like crumpled tissue paper, as if torn apart. Ji-ae hurriedly went into the bath as if to chase away his apparition and turned on the water. Gushing forth, the aluminum lips released a fierce stream of water. Still, she slid her foot beneath the chilly stream and gradually submerged herself, starting from her feet, then knees, and finally sinking into the depths of the tub. The water grew warmer gradually. Adjusting the temperature, she let her entire body soak under the gentle cascade of the shower. As the moisture touched her skin from head to toe, her cells jolted in surprise, assuming a rigid posture. The tiny insects that had been squirming and writhing in desire suddenly relaxed and raised their hands in surrender. Slowly, they acquiesced. The water was now completely cold. The once placid cells shivered in shock, braving the chill. Goosebumps formed like the tip of a hypodermic needle. After standing in the cold water for a while, she stepped out of the tub and dried herself off. It was over now. At least the precarious acrobatics of her flesh tormenting her throughout the day had come to an end. With a refreshed spirit, she hurried off to work. Memories of last night's gathering at Hyun's coffee shop flooded her mind. When she arrived at Mi-young's after seven, there were already half a dozen young men and women gathered, chatting and enjoying pastries.

'My mom is too interfering, my dad is incompetent, and he always opposes anything American. He always says Koreans should be like this or that. If I say anything even a little, I'm met with disapproval. I can't understand my dad's words. I don't even know how to become a Korean.' A high school girl with long hair down to her shoulders said. 'That's right, Yeong-hee's right. It's difficult to just blindly follow the idea of 'you don't know, you should obey your parents.' If that's Korean style, I won't follow it. We really need to have a conversation,' said a male student sitting in the corner with his legs on the table. 'We talk, but our parents block the conversation and only assert themselves. I don't know if our parents even know what a conversation is,' another student blurted out. Hyun silently listened to the children's conversation. From their conversation, the students gathered there could all sense that there were problems in their homes or schools. It was pitiful. However, amidst the pity, a wind blew into her. It was a warm wind. Just a little more patience, a little more strength. Right now, even the parents are clueless, you're stumbling around like children, but it will end. As time goes by, we will come to discern where we stand." This seems to be a passage from a Korean text, perhaps a novel or a piece of literature. Let me know if you need further assistance!

After that, we will hold hands and move forward.' Finally, Hyun talked about the differences between her parents' upbringing and the hardships of early immigrant life in a culture with different language and customs. Then, she emphasized the need to try to understand parents from their perspective and never to let go of the thread of conversation. She also said, '... I know this may sound like mere speculation. But I don't know of any better prescription yet. Until the doctor knows a better prescription, they must use the best prescription within their knowledge for the patient, right?' With an unruffled attitude, he looked around at each of them. A sense of solemnity was capturing their attention. Ji-ae sensed a deep and intimate connection between him and them and looked at him again with renewed admiration. Where did that strength come from? After the gathering, as students poured out in a rush, Hyun stopped two kids. 'Yeong-hee, are you not going to school?' he asked, looking towards the girl. 'School? Why would I go to school? There's nothing to learn. It's just a place where I feel annoyed and want to die. Why would I go there?' 'Yeong-hee will be okay. Don't worry, teacher.'

Standing next to her, Sang-ho wrapped his arm around Yeong-hee's shoulder and added as they were about to leave, 'Yeong-hee will also find a job.' His eyes watching their retreating figures carried deep concern. 'The students I mentioned earlier. They seem to have bolted from their homes,' he said after taking a long breath. 'Would you like something to eat? Thank you for coming out tonight. You both said some good things. What's important to them is the trust that someone cares about them. Like waiting for rain in a drought, they stretch their necks, waiting for someone's attention. Their hearts are eager. They respond readily even to small gestures of interest.' 'That's not true. You're really doing a good thing, teacher.' Mi-young looked at him with admiration. 'No, let's stop with that. I'm just try-ing to be their friend, to provide a space where they can gather and express themselves,' he said. 'How important is that? If complaints against parents or irrational grievances are left unaddressed, they'll become time bombs ready to explode later on, won't they?'

Mi-young had said something similar to them. 'All this started from a very chance event. That student I helped in court earlier? That's the kid. It seemed like he couldn't get himself together after-ward, so I suggested he come out with friends.' 'Ah, I see.' Ji-ae and Mi-young said simultaneously. 'Haha, would you like something to eat? I'm quite skilled at this, you know.' He awkwardly laughed and gestured for them to sit. Mi-young gave Ji-ae a meaningful glance. He prepared orange juice and simple snacks for the women. Ji-ae wasn't very hungry with the snacks the kids brought, but eating the vegetable and meat omelet he made gave her a thrilling sensation.

Why does he live like this? If he had quit being a priest, wouldn't he be solving human loneliness with his family by now? 'Is living amusing?' he asked as he drove, dropping off Mi-young in Manhattan first and then taking Ji-ae to Flushing, Queens. 'Not really.' 'I've been quite curious. How have you been?'"

Ji-ae seemed to perceive from his tone a precarious balancing act, as if he was trying to maintain a delicate distance between them. 'I felt the same way.' 'Look at that river. The waves are so serene, yet people's hearts are so harsh. It feels like they're living as if today is the only day, and tomorrow they must leave for somewhere far away. That's our immigrant society.' 'It will get better soon. I want to believe that. It's just the early stages of unpacking,' Ji-ae reflected on her own words. 'Those students from earlier, are they all recent immigrant students?' 'Mostly, yes. Children whose parents run businesses or work. Kids like Sang-ho have fathers who own big liquor stores.' 'But...' The car continued towards White Stone Bridge even after passing Ji-ae's apartment complex. 'Ji-ae, would you like to take a drive with me?' he said without stopping the car. 'Sure.'

He parked the car at a riverside spot overlooking White Stone Bridge, connecting the Bronx and Queens. There were factories or dilapidated buildings nearby, and behind them, tall mugwort fields stood shoulder to shoulder with reed beds. The mugwort fields seemed to stand still, listening to the tales brought by the wind from all over the world. He turned off the engine and looked at Ji-ae. Ji-ae didn't avoid his gaze. A tiny spark flickered in her dark and stifled heart. Beneath the deep and thick layers of consciousness, a bird chirped, fluttering its wings. He got out of the car and held Ji-ae's hand, still sitting inside, leading her outside. Passing through the reeds and mugwort fields standing between the river and the houses, they stood side by side facing the river. The moonlight gently shimmered on the river, and the river cautiously reflected the light. Across the river, the mammoth buildings of Manhattan's downtown area stood proudly, adorned with jewels like a lady's evening gown, towering into the night sky. Some buildings emitted faint light, while others, towering tall, became a cluster of jewels. 'Isn't it beautiful? The nights of Manhattan seen from here feel like stars falling from the sky, performing magic on the ground.' His tone became notably lighter.

'Indeed, it's truly beautiful. I didn't know such a place existed, even though I've lived nearby for so long.' After a moment of silence, he spoke as if lost in thought. 'After I finished law school, I enlisted in the military soon after. After my discharge, I briefly attended university and then went to Vietnam as a war correspondent. I wondered if I could escape my own incompetence in Vietnam. At that time, I only saw my own ego and tried to think of myself like a foot stepping on the burning embers.' '...' 'What happened in Vietnam was their suffering, not ours. The blood shed was by the Vietnamese. Ji-ae, how much do you think humans can participate in others' miseries? The tragedy of humanity lies in the fact that no one can bear the burden of others' suffering as their own. Humanity is cruel and deceitful. Humanity's despair stems from its inability to break through its own hypocrisy.' Ji-ae couldn't look at him. From him, she heard the sound of a wounded bird. 'Ah, when did I start hearing that sound? 'Like building sandcastles on the beach, little by little we build the castle of humanity, but when the tide comes rushing in, the once passionate fervor cools off. It's no different from children playing with sand on the beach.' Ji-ae thought of her cousin, who had vigorously protested the government in college and now enjoyed a lavish life at the center of Seoul as a high-ranking government official."

'Ji-ae, I got to know those students there. I had the opportunity to befriend a university professor teaching at Saigon University, and through him, I happened to sit with the young people once. They were as innocent as young people from any country. Ho Chi Minh dug caves on the Cambodia-Vietnam border to provide ideological education to 100,000 young people. Those who opposed his ideology were all killed, and those who sympathized were forced into labor camps for ideological education. The young man I met was one of those who escaped from the forced labor camp. Unlike the authorities who only had eyes for their power even in the face of Ho Chi Minh's sword and bombs, they were true patriots. Every time I see this flowing river, I think of the Mekong River. I can't forget the young man named Don who escaped with patriotism in his heart to the Mekong River, rather than dying by Ho Chi Minh's sword. I still remember his poem.' 'To your earth and dust, adorned with my comrades' blood, oh homeland, today I offer my life at your altar of freedom. I pour out my last drops of rain, offering my love.'

'Their ultimate sacrifice for freedom came at such a heavy price. It was the sorrow of being born as a minority youth. To them, freedom was a grudge ingrained in their bones. I realized how precious freedom and homeland were back then. A nation without a country... My thoughts lingered on that, and my heart bled.' '...!' 'Ji-ae, I thought of our 38th parallel back then. How much better and farther could someone run with one leg compared to those who ran with both legs? How much difference could there be between those running with one leg and those running with both? But back then, I also thought about how having hope could be a source of strength. Our homeland may be divided by the 38th parallel, but the hope that reunification will come someday, the assurance that there is that homeland, firmly planted my resolve.' Ji-ae remembered the Prague incident. She silently recalled how anxious and fearful she had been at that time. Perhaps history could start with miracles and end with miracles. Look, the history of Israel, breaking free from the chains of slavery in Egypt, crossing the Red Sea, and conquering Canaan. She had listened to her grandfather's stories countless times when she was young and had found them fascinating like fairy tales. Her grandfather had been so serious. 'Ji-ae, the splitting of the Red Sea is a recorded fact in world history.'

After Ji-ae grew up, her grandfather had even proclaimed it as a historical fact. Yes, looking at human history from a human perspective, it could be full of paradoxes, mysteries, and perhaps even coincidences. How sorrowful it must have been for the Israelites, a nation without a country for 2000 years... Such thoughts bubbled up like foam. Was it just them, just Israel? Who fans the flames of history? Is it the wind, or the unseen hand of the wind? Ji-ae found herself nodding slightly without realizing it. It was such a meaningless gesture, an attempt to shake off her thoughts. 'Ji-ae, looking at them, I realized that our homeland isn't just a piece of land; it's the hope and hearts of the people held within. The homeland resides in the blood and hearts of the nation; the land itself is just a symbol, overwhelmed by fire. When the hopes of the people's hearts cannot be fulfilled, or rather, when their hearts are trampled upon, then that land ceases to be a symbol of the homeland... And there's the tragedy of having to fight against one's own people, even to the point of death, as in Vietnam.' He finished speaking and fell into silence. After a while, as if dreaming, he spoke again. 'Ji-ae, have you ever thought? Honest and truthful patriots driven by conscience, leaders who stand with the nation and the people in the face of tragedy, without turning a blind eye but standing together in truth.

"Ji-ae, I'm sorry for saying this. But my experience there was truly shocking. Even now, when I silently watch this flowing river, it feels like I can hear their cries. The voices of those who screamed and pleaded with their throats hoarse, their desperate struggles as they jumped into the sea, rocking to ride the boats. I think it became a more powerful rhetoric than any politician's speech, any bomb, shaking the conscience of the world. The problem is that the picture is gradually being erased. Ji-ae, when a country disappears from this earth, it means that not only the long history of that country but also the blood, hearts, and pain shed for that country are erased meaninglessly. That's where the tragedy lies, isn't it?" Ji-ae shook her head as she listened to his words. "No, Hyun, you're wrong. That blood, those hearts, that pain, they don't disappear. They remain as nourishment for humanity to continue living." Hyun's words echoed dreamily. "I'm accusing myself now. Above all, the world must not forget Vietnam's final tragedy. We must not bury the cries of blood, the cries of those who shouted their last breaths for freedom, in the Mekong River and wipe our mouths. We must not let such tragedy happen again. But that's exactly what we, the superpowers, are doing now. Ji-ae, that's where the problem lies. History repeats itself if we forget it, a terrifying fact."

Ji-ae listened to his words and suddenly felt a tightness in her chest. "But it's all so chaotic. Unthinkable things keep happening in the world, and why do people have to suffer............ It's unfair. What losing a country means, why it's such a despairing tragedy..." Ji-ae paused. "Of course, my hometown and my homeland are both deeply ingrained in my heart, making me feel lonely and sometimes engulfed in a vague sense of longing, but it's become part of my existence." Ji-ae thought about it, quietly wanting to just listen to his words and feel comfortable. But Ji-ae pondered his words deeply. Was he right? Though he didn't say it, following his logic, when a country disappears from this land, does it mean that the hopes, love, and traditions of the people who were with it for so long also disappear? If so, the world would be impoverished by that much. If one part is torn away, it becomes incomplete and lacking, and if it's the fountain of prosperity for the world, it can't make a big circle, so it becomes everyone's, no, all of our misfortune.

But Ji-ae rebelled, saying, "Hyun, you're wrong. Those things never disappear. Never, ever. Is human history eternal?" Hyun, who had been silent, said, "Of course, history shouldn't be seen up close; it should be seen from afar. Only after seeing it from afar, looking at it long, can we grasp the meaning of the pain and hope of an era." Ji-ae thought. How serious must it have been for him to repeat it like this? If she held his hands, laid her head on his chest and shoulders, could she comfort him? Ah, for a moment, a boat passed by on the calm river, causing ripples. The slightly tilted crescent moon looked down faintly to the west. He turned to Ji-ae. "Ji-ae, it's truly amazing. That I can relieve the frustration in my heart to Ji-ae like this again! I thought I would never meet Ji-ae again. In the midst of war, with death looming before me, the desperation to meet Ji-ae just once..." His voice was getting louder. Ji-ae looked at him. His face, which still seemed to want to say something more, an awkward face, felt like if she opened the door, the things piled up in that room, no, some desperate word, would pour out like a landslide.

However, his face reveals only faint contours in the moonlit greenish-blue light. "Ji-ae, the reason I didn't return to Korea but came to the United States is...?? Whoever among you is without sin, let them cast the first stone at this woman." He was sitting on the author's street, writing. The place he was writing was not on the ground but on a stone field. The words carved into the stone field were blood. People did not retreat. They mocked and threw stones closer to him. Just as if they were arguing, both you and the woman cursed him. The woman cried out in pain on his knees. She clung to his clothes. He held the dead woman in his arms. His face momentarily resembled Hyun's face. It was a dream. His whole body was soaked in sweat. Ji-ae got up, took a shower, and drank hot tea, reflecting on what Hyun had said last Saturday night. How far does his suffering go? Why should he hurt so much? What happened in a foreign country he couldn't bear, holding it in his chest and struggling. In India, they feed poisonous mushrooms to people to make them feel empty and find a new self in that emptiness... In the morning, Mi-young visited Ji-ae's office. "Did you go home well?" She asked, looking at Ji-ae's reaction.

"Huh?" "Last Saturday night." "Yeah." "What kind of answer is that?" Mi-young suddenly glared at Ji-ae, showing irritation. Who scolded Mi-young in her mind. 'Mi-young, I'm sorry. It seems like you like Hyun. Ji-ae found it strange that Mi-young, who was staring intently at him, said that. "Why are you like this?" "I went to a revival meeting last night." "Oh my, look at this. When did you become so devout?" "The problem is I can't rush into faith like them. Last night, I couldn't resist the long-standing persuasion of a high school classmate living nearby. I looked at their bright faces and wondered where it came from, why I couldn't do that. I thought of the preacher's words. You must meet God, the problem is that I can't meet the personal Him... That's what it means to truly be reborn. That's a changed person, and if not, going to church is the same, saying similar things. Believing in an unseen presence, that's the problem, hahaha..." Oh, what's her concern? Ji-ae felt a pang in his heart as he listened to Mi-young's unprecedented words and saw her anguish. After Mi-young left and Ji-ae was cooling his head with coffee, he received a call from Hyun.

Ji-ae finished work and Hyun greeted him with a smile as he walked out. He drove down the highway to Brooklyn. Bathed in the warm light of the fiery twilight, the World Trade Center in southern Manhattan was shimmering side by side. Ji-ae felt out his side until then as he silently held the steering wheel. Lips tightly shut, his intellectual eyes drawing lines softly to the side, and a suitably high bridge of the nose. With that as the center, his eyes harmonized gently with the masculine facial lines. That face said a lot. I don't know if I love him because of that face. Love carves the other into a mystery, they say, and love is drawn to the abyss of the mystery it carves. Where to? I saw the Statue of Liberty holding a torch on top of a gray island, with dimly lit islands and ash-colored buildings far away. Send me those who long for tired and poor freedom on the coast there, those who are brutally abandoned without homes and tired from storms.

"I'll light the lantern by the golden gate for you, America is a country that ignites a fire of ideals, not just for itself, but for the whole world. Knowledge, bankruptcy, even freedom, and love... What about now? Are people still flocking here in search of dreams they couldn't achieve in their own countries? Is America still opening its arms warmly to those without homes, tired from storms? To Ji-ae, such things now seemed like a political show and not his sincere gestures. "Someone said that. Once you turn this corner, you've seen all of New York." He said without looking back at Ji-ae. "Really? From here, it's beautiful to see Manhattan where the Hudson and East rivers meet and join the Atlantic." Nearby, the Verrazzano-Narrows Bridge connecting Brooklyn and Staten Island could be seen. "That bridge is the longest and highest in the world. Although putting the best on something is ultimately relative." Flocks of seagulls gathered low over the sea and then suddenly soared into the air. Fearlessly crossing the highway. The waves, once burning with golden light, gradually turned yellow and began to cast shadows of darkness.

"Ji-ae, are you not hungry?" He said as he parked the car near the Fulton Fish Market waterfront. "It's a busy time when people gather if they're coming in with a boatload of fish straight from the sea." "It reminds me of a small harbor in Italy." Ji-ae said. "When I'm here, it feels like my stuffy heart is being pushed back a century." "Do you come here often?" "No. Once, I closed the shop in the evening and ended up walking along the Hudson River and ended up by the sea. It felt enveloping. The people on this street looked different, even the waitress seemed friendlier and more relaxed." A nearby restaurant with a large fish painted on it was entered. Despite it not being the weekend, there were many people having a party. But they were all Asians. "Do you have contact with Korea?" He asked suddenly, sitting at a table by the window where they were previously silent. "Contact with Korea?" "No, not at all."

"Has it always been like this?" "Always." Ji-ae turned his gaze out the window. "I'm sorry. For asking such questions..." "... Mi-young said that your husband hasn't had any contact since returning home." "No, he came once." The aftermath of the stones he threw and left resurfaced from his last visit. His mother, left alone, gazes at the southern sky every day, resting her hand on her chest... Some say that she walks along the Han River, back and forth between north and south... She was still beautiful, but her rough, stone-like palms made me happy. I couldn't resist those harsh palms. And inevitably, we ended up living together... Ji-ae shook off those thoughts like erasing wrong words with an eraser and turned his head out the window. A seagull, flying peacefully in the dense sea fog, fluttered and fell. He doubted what Hyun had said through Mi-young. Why did Mi-young say that? Ji-ae felt ashamed at that moment. Is he building a wall between the years he has lived and his relationship with Hyun?... My shameful life will disappear someday. Like that seagull. She whispered to herself. No, the time I've lived won't disappear like that. The footprints I've left will fossilize in time and remain.

Along with the pain of my soul. But what am I? Hyun was pained by the suffering of a foreign country he encountered last time. Despite his denial, that pain would have left a noble mark, enriching his soul. Then, what am I? Who was it that said, "God loved mankind so much that He made no two people alike, and within each, He carved a dream just for them?" Yes, perhaps I am destined to wander in search of that dream all my life. What path am I on? The air was fresh and soft. The scent of the mudflats filled my nostrils. After dinner, I stepped out onto the dock. The fishing boats, like heads of families returning from a long journey to the embrace of their loving homes, rested proudly at the dock. Some emitted a soft, lantern-like glow, while others lay quietly, their dim bodies at rest. Ji-ae wanted to spend the night on one of these boats, with him. No, to sleep deeply and comfortably in his arms like a baby... To never wake up again would be a blissful, eternal rest there. With him, it seems I could forget everything. The worries about my husband's affairs and occasional distress concerning him, too.

Accompanied by her own reproach and guilt, Ji-ae parked the car in front of her house, and he graciously opened the car door for her. "Good night," he said. "Thank you," she replied, pausing briefly in front of him. She then turned and ascended the steps to her home. Looking back from the door, he was still standing there. Ji-ae gestured for him to go, but he remained motionless. Standing against the backlight of a streetlamp, his expression was unreadable. She turned the key weakly and opened the door, glancing back at him. Only then did he raise his hand and disappear into the car. Ji-ae pressed the switch beside the door with an uncertain hand. As the house lit up, the furniture that had been crouching in the darkness gradually began to reveal itself. They seemed unfamiliar, almost as if they resisted her presence, cold and distant. Could it really be that her own home, filled with objects touched by her own hands, could feel so alien? Ji-ae collapsed onto a chair. In her dreams, she was with Hyun by the seaside. The waves surged high overhead before settling back down as if to sleep. Seagulls lazily flew above them. Hand in hand, they walked along the beach, running endlessly. Barefoot and playful, the waves thoroughly erased their footprints left in the sandy beach.

"Ji-ae, even the traces of human existence, the marks of human history, they all disappear as time goes by. Time is cruel. Time is not on the side of humans. No, it isn't. Haha!" He laughed like a madman and lifted Ji-ae high in the air. Like a ball. She felt empty and weightless like the wind. Ji-ae chuckled. Embracing his neck, pressing her face against his, they soared through the sky like a well-rehearsed duet of dancers. Somewhere far away. Where there's a shooting star, warm and bright. Higher than the stars, beyond the galaxies, beyond the vast expanse of the universe, there was a dazzling endless city in his mind. Her heart swelled with emotion. "Oh, it's so beautiful, so beautiful, radiant and ecstatic! I want to live there. Hyun, with you, forever." Ji-ae exclaimed like a child, pulling Hyun closer. "This is what freedom is, freedom is something pure and without a trace of greed, shining with endless peace." Hyun's resonant voice echoed from all directions. He chuckled softly. His flawless laughter surged like waves, overflowing with light. It flowed beyond the universe. With the sound echoing even louder, he disappeared along with it. Ji-ae was left alone on the beach. Clutching the cold sand, she was alone. It's been almost a month since she met Mi-young. She hasn't heard from Hyun since they had dinner together at the dock. Ji-ae waited for Hyun's call. She felt superficially sorry for Mi-young.

Mi-young deliberately avoiding her... It was Friday afternoon. Ji-ae got up from seeing a patient and went to the window to cool her head when the phone rang. "Ji-ae!" "You called!" Her voice trembled. "Well, meet me in front of the hospital later." Ji-ae quietly put down the receiver. She checked the clock. It was four o'clock, an hour from now! To her, that hour felt like eternity. At exactly five o'clock, as she stepped out of the hospital door, he was already there, waiting. Sitting in a light blue car, when he saw Ji-ae, he got out of the car and opened the door for her. "Where shall we go?" "Wherever you'd like, Hyun." "Alright. There's a small restaurant by the Brooklyn beach. It's not far." The late afternoon light of late summer was gentle. Sitting beside him in the car, Ji-ae felt the twenty years of separation and reunion with him seemed both eternal and momentary, which struck her as strange. "What are you thinking?"

Ji-ae felt his tone was somewhat comical. "Um, I was thinking about that evening when I met you, Hyun." Ji-ae's face turned red. "Ah, I see. I was actually thinking about that too." A faint laughter passed between them as they looked at each other. They settled in at a cozy Italian-style restaurant by the Brooklyn beach. Looking around the interior, Ji-ae remarked, "Do you think this place will do well?" "Well, those people are well-off... You don't see it today, but sometimes the owner's wife comes out and they work together." The owner greeted them warmly and came to take their order. Without much wait, they were served grilled fish with vegetables and soup. As Ji-ae ate the grilled fish facing him, she wondered why he was alone, a silly thought. He still hadn't mentioned his personal life. "It's very quiet here." His voice sounded distant, as if in a dream. Ji-ae, as if trying to tackle a difficult homework assignment, hesitated as she spoke. "Why... didn't you... get married, Hyun?" In an instant, Hyun's eyes widened as he looked at Ji-ae, then he looked away. Ji-ae felt guilty. She wanted to cry. "Let's stop talking about our past. The food will get cold." It seemed as if she was trying to break the awkward silence that followed.

He smoothed his voice and said, "America is a melting pot. At least for us Koreans, it is. They don't force you to have a changed face or a fake one." Ji-ae thought of Shim Minguk, whom she met last Christmas. He had said it was hard to change jobs, but he had recently informed her that he had opened a laundromat with his wife and was working hard for his children. He laughed heartily... "Freedom is truly important, especially for us Koreans. Our ancestors shed blood and sacrificed their lives and prosperity under Japanese rule for freedom as if offering up their own bodies. We are their descendants." His conversation took a leap. Suddenly, he stopped talking and focused on a point above Ji-ae's head. Ji-ae looked at him quietly. His serene and tranquil eyes, his soft lips, were tightly closed in a straight line. After finishing their meal and leaving a tip, he said, "Ji-ae. Shall we go out for a walk?" Without waiting for Ji-ae's answer, he stood up. They walked along the beach. A small hill appeared. There, a bench facing the sea was placed. He spread his coat over it and gestured for Ji-ae to sit. The wind blew, carrying the moisture of the sea and the scent of the mudflats, brushing past their noses.

"Are you cold?" Ji-ae tilted her head. "Oh, it feels like a dream. To be able to meet you like this, Ji-ae!" Ji-ae kept repeating apologies in her mind. She didn't even know what they meant, as the strong waves crashed against the beach and receded. Seagulls fluttered away, chasing after the waves. "I've never forgotten a single day in the past twenty years. Even when I returned from Vietnam to my homeland, it was ultimately because of the thought of meeting Ji-ae. But why couldn't I meet Ji-ae, who lived right next door at that time..." I knew. The day I first saw Ji-ae at the farewell party, everything became clear. I've always regretted it. Why didn't I hold on to Ji-ae? Even if it was just the day we last met on that hill before graduation, the day of our last gathering... I was such a fool back then." "At that time, you had decided to go to Germany..." "A bride? When I heard that Ji-ae had left for the United States, I realized that I was not suitable to be her husband." "Why, why not?" "Don't ask that question. It's not something that can be explained easily. One thing is clear: when I met Ji-ae for the first time at the student circle, I felt like a new world was opening up to me. But at that time, everything was unclear to me."

"After Ji-ae left, I was overwhelmed with despair at losing her forever and with the guilt of not being worthy to be her husband. The reasons were unclear, but..." "...?" "After that, I couldn't be okay with anyone." "I couldn't be happy either. I always remembered your words, Hyun, that last word, 'be happy,' clinging to those words..." He turned to Ji-ae with a newfound seriousness. His eyes were filled with profound compassion. "The world without Ji-ae was a wandering and empty one for me. Endless wandering... And then, strangely, God seemed to give me a small reprimand. It was truly bizarre. Using the word 'punishment' in such a case!"

From the Valley of Death

"It was one night under a brightly shining full moon, a night that gave off a truly eerie feeling. Unable to sleep, I had left the barracks and was sitting under a tree, lost in my own thoughts. Suddenly, I heard a rustling sound from somewhere—no, right behind me. Instinctively, I quickly hid behind the tree and stared in the direction of the noise. My heart was racing uncontrollably, and guess who I thought of in that moment? Ji-ae, it was you. The Ji-ae I envisioned had a face filled with despair and torment. Then, a Vietnamese woman appeared from between the bushes, carrying something on her back. I held my breath as I watched her approach. She was carrying something that resembled a bundle on her back, her hands pressed together in a gesture of begging as she approached. Unconsciously, I moved toward the woman. She kept pointing at her back, continuing her desperate gestures. When I looked at her back, it was a child. A dead child. It seemed she did not even know her child had died, and had ventured into the night risking her life to seek help. Not far from where we were encamped, there was a village where the Vietnamese civilians had chosen not to flee but to stay."

It appeared she had come from there. Just then, an officer emerged from the barracks. He pushed me aside with fierce anger and dragged the woman inside. Even then, she was covering her back with her hands, spouting unclear Vietnamese words. But the officer was relentless. As they disappeared into the barracks, I too entered. "What happened to that woman afterward?" "It was the next morning. I went outside because it was bustling. Surrounded by our troops, the woman from the previous night was trembling with terror, holding a child." "Eliminate her! What are you doing!" a muffled voice snapped impatiently. It was the officer from yesterday. "She's not a guerrilla, is she?" someone protested. "It's an order. It doesn't matter. Just do it. How can you trust her?" "But..." The tension between the two was palpable, and the harsh Vietnamese sun seemed to scorch the air yellow. "Sergeant Kim! Don't you know that sentimentality is self-destructive for a soldier? We must prepare for any contingency. Just do it. What are you doing?" Commanded by the fiery officer, he reluctantly prepared himself. By then, the woman, who had been trembling with fear, seemed to realize what was happening.

Only then, as if resigned, she bowed her body and held her dead child tightly. Then a gunshot rang out, and she collapsed, covered in rags. "Oh, it can't be! No matter the war!" "In situations where there's little difference between life and death, there's no right for humans to be human. What could Ji-ae think there?" "The aftermath of war is often more terrifying for an individual than experiencing it firsthand. The death of that woman for her child's sake, and the freedom she sought, drove her to just jump into the water, leaving a few bubbles behind, like so many Vietnamese..." With a crackle, the highway lights shattered under the hazy waves. Several seagulls, perhaps missing humans or the sea, circled above, diving down under the crashing waves below the rocky shore and rising again. The seagulls repeated it like a crucial refrain in a song. "Shall we go?" His determined voice echoed. Ji-ae wasn't cold, nor did he want to leave. Time, please stop, for the perennially pained human voice through his lips becomes a lullaby putting my soul to rest.

Ji-ae took a moment to contemplate the world he had left behind. The lonely, restless nights awaiting him after parting ways. The mundane tasks at the hospital, where he had to confront all sorts of people. He hesitated. He didn't want to get up. He didn't want to face the cruel world that stripped his soul bare. The reality of forcing himself back into the shell terrified him. As he tried to rise, he hesitated again and sat back down. "Some time later, when we were retaking a hill and coming back to the base, we saw something hanging from the trees in the forest as we descended the hill. It was evening. We went closer." He seemed like a person in a dream. "They were human corpses. Not Vietnamese soldiers, but over a dozen corpses, uniformly ragged and dirty, of women and children, and an old man.

It was the doing of the Viet Cong fleeing. They weren't shot, but impaled with spears, holes in their throats and bellies spilling out intestines. Ji-ae, at that moment, I felt like I was standing at the gates of hell. The stench of decaying bodies pierced my nose from those still warm with heat, somewhere the faint breath of humans' final moments could be heard... Crows were cawing madly above them. We covered our noses and fled as if escaping death itself. Following suit, I trembled in disgust and despair at what it means to be human."

"It was night. That night, I inexplicably went back there. I don't know why I went alone that night. I shivered as I saw bodies hanging from branches. My rationality and emotions swayed, engulfed by pitch darkness. Then, without realizing it, I lost my mind and aimed my gun at my head in the dim moonlight. Dying seemed so simple then. But suddenly, I felt a strong force holding my hand. Unknowingly, I dropped the gun and fell to my knees. The force of inevitability... The darkness that was just there disappeared, and light enveloped my entire body. Light, sweetness, the light of hope seen from the depths of despair, ah, the light beyond Kierkegaard's despair, that light. Strangely, in that moment, I saw Christ's blood on their footprints. It's a truly bizarre paradox, isn't it, Ji-ae? There was only sweetness there. I couldn't feel anything. The tragic forest of Vietnam where I sat, and my endlessly torn existence, even the madness of death... In the midst of that blood, there was Christ on the cross. Ah, he was real. Ji-ae, he was real!" His long reminiscence seemed like a murky echo to Ji-ae. The wind blew. The hazy waves murmured like a band. Perhaps the sea had a crust like a turtle shell, breaking it and coming out, dreaming of a quiet emergency as if spitting out swallowed leftovers.

Ji-ae followed his gaze towards the horizon. The soundless words of wisdom seemed to echo to Ji-ae as well. Something like the whispers of language resonated in her heart. Was everything originated from that sea, that endless sea? Was it from beneath the endless sea where the vast and expansive human mind was born, even greater than the universe? Yes, the sea is the chorus of language, the home of language. Perhaps there is a place of creation there. And the beginning of time..." Ji-ae seemed to be dreaming. The sea holds all the beginnings and ends of humanity quietly unfolded before them. The desolate war in Vietnam, the futile end of the war, the tragic fate of a divided homeland, now seemed to have only conclusions there, only endings. Equality and peace alone... How much time had passed? He broke the silence. "Ji-ae." His voice tone became tighter and higher. Like seawater surging over a rock protruding from the beach. "Ji-ae, do you understand?" "...?"

"Human history is a spectacle. Human history is the spectacle of the powerful." Ji-ae turned to look at him. His profile was blotched like a canvas soaked in light and darkness. "Ji-ae, do you understand? It's a tremendous fact, a truth. On the stage of the powerful, the jesters dance for their own power, blinded to the plight of those struggling for life, impoverished and unjust, they don't see the actions behind the curtain, the cries of agony beneath the stage. The greed of the jesters on the stage is too loud. Their dance is too magnificent." ...?? "The problem lies there. They are so intoxicated by their antics that they deem it righteous and boast of their competence." "......" "Truth falls like autumn leaves, scattered from the altar of crops. History is sustained by the voices of the unrecorded, the unheard words held in silence. That is the truth and the fact." Hyun's dreamy yet quiet voice trembled. His voice pulled Ji-ae back to reality. Only then did Ji-ae realize that his shoulders were cold. The chill air came from the sea, escaping from the highway's rushing wheels and the slopes of the beach.

Ah, Hyun. If I could lull you to sleep, cradle you in my arms like a baby, gently stroke your heavy head soaked in anguish to soothe you to sleep, if I could embrace your soul like a mother embracing a baby swaddled in comfort... Hyun, for the sake of human spirit, as the one who bore the cross on your shoulders of consciousness, who are you? Who are you? Ji-ae trembled.

Coffee Shop

"Good morning, Mr. Jin." Robert Pinkenstein, who had been waiting outside until the door opened, entered. "Hello? Did you sleep well last night, Mr. Pinkenstein?" "Oh, yes, yes!" The old man replied with a meaningless answer, his face breaking into a sheepish smile. Mr. Jin brewed coffee and served the old man. His shop, which opened at six in the morning, always began the day with meetings between him and the old man like this. "Mr. Jin, are you feeling unwell? You don't look well. You seem to be not feeling well lately, why is that?" "Oh, it's nothing. Thank you for your concern." At that moment, he thought of Ji-ae. And he remembered the confession he made to her on the beach ten days ago. If he had come to New York to find her and met her, it would have been even better...."

The tension of overlapping bodies after unexpectedly meeting her at the year-end party. Since parting ways with Ji-ae and returning, he had developed a habit of tossing and turning in bed, unable to sleep, often staying up late flipping through books. "This won't do. I need to start exercising again." He muttered to himself as he went to the storage room to grab a mop and started cleaning the floor. "Mr. Jin, we'll just have breakfast for two here, please." A young couple, who had come in unnoticed, sat at a table ready for breakfast. Ever since coming to New York, he had taken up the business upon his friend's insistence, and he readily catered to the meal orders of his customers. As he disposed of the food scraps in the trash bin, Sang-ho and Yeong-hee walked in. "What's going on, up so early." He commented, examining their faces closely. Yeong-hee's face spoke volumes. "Yeong-hee, are you feeling unwell?" "No." Yeong-hee replied briefly, lowering her head. "Are you doing well at work?" He turned to Sang-ho. "I quit my job." Sang-ho replied dully.

"She doesn't want to do that kind of work. She doesn't want to hear her boss nagging, or stick to a schedule." "Then what about Sang-ho?" "Me?" "He still hasn't gone home." "Looks like he's in trouble now." He felt strangely unsettled by Yeong-hee's vague answer. What have these guys done? "Did Sung-jin know about it? Sung-jin called. Seems like he's doing well. He's going to college to study engineering." "......" "Just let him be. Sung-jin came in the same year as you guys." "He has different parents." Sang-ho raised his voice nervously. The guests looked at them. "I'm sorry, sir. We're busy." Just then, a flamboyantly dressed middle-aged Caucasian woman entered, winking at him with one eye. She was a regular customer, although somewhat absent-mindedly bothersome at times. "Hi, Ms. Homkister." "Good morning, Jinhyun, I hope you have what I'm looking for." She grinned at him.

He gestured for Sang-ho and Yeong-hee to wait, then went to fetch the lunch fries the woman had ordered before returning to the young couple. "Are you keeping in touch with your parents?" "We meet them occasionally." Sang-ho replied indifferently, turning his head away. Hyun, feeling somewhat intoxicated, remembered Sang-ho's father, who always seemed flushed and volatile, for some reason Sang-ho's birth mother remained in Korea while he lived here with another woman. "He's a good-for-nothing son. Why, what's lacking that he had to run away from home? He wants me to see him for work? Just stick around at home or go to school." Speaking with a heavy mix of Gyeongsang Province dialect, he bluntly berated Sang-ho as if he were confronting him face to face. As he looked around the store, filled with bottles of various colors like a festival, Hyun collided with an invisible wall. He had gone to reconcile with Sang-ho's father, but he couldn't overcome the insurmountable barrier himself, and he bit back a sigh in his mouth. He had seen it. "But if his father speaks well to him, Sang-ho has good character and will listen well. It's just the fiery passion of youth..." "What are you telling me to do? Should I bow to my child? If he had been taken out and thrown into a juvenile detention center or something and then brought back, that would have been enough. I just let it go."

He poured out his resentment towards his son, struggling to find the words. How could such an obstinate person have come all the way to America? How could he explain that money doesn't solve everything to someone who thinks it does? "Then, I'll come back." Sang-ho put his arm around Yeong-hee's shoulder and left. "Keep in touch often. If anything, even tonight..." He seemed somewhat bitter. Even ominous thoughts crept in. Those guys must have done something wrong. Yeong-hee was strange. It was three years ago, wasn't it? As he was about to close the shop for the day, a young man standing outside suddenly pulled out a knife and thrust it at him. He stepped back in surprise and looked around quickly. Fortunately, there was no one nearby. He looked the intruder in the face. Perhaps intimidated by his authority, the young man with the knife trembled and bowed his head. "Hey, you look like a Korean student, why are you doing this? Let's go inside." He brought the unexpected intruder inside. It turned out to be Sang-ho. Since then, Sang-ho had gotten into trouble with a Chinese gang and had run afoul of the police. After that incident, he had tried to comfort Sang-ho and reach out to other troubled kids, trying to be their mental support, but he always hesitated. Could he do what parents and society couldn't? Self-doubt followed him like a shadow.

Initially, they used empty spaces like apartment staircases for their activities, but now they've managed to rent a room where six of them live together. The problem of neglected youth, like discarded cigarette butts. Where does all the money in the Korean community go? He keenly feels the need for some organized institution for the youth nowadays.

"Yeong-hee's Death

Teacher, I'm sorry. But I couldn't help it. But I couldn't go home either. I didn't even want to go. If I went in like this, our dad would probably break my legs. Teacher, more than that, I didn't want to bring shame to my parents. Of course, if I go like this, they'll be sad for a while. Sadness doesn't last that long. They'll be okay. I thought about seeing you one more time, but I was afraid I'd lose my resolve, so I decided to write a letter instead. Teacher, goodbye. Thank you for everything. If there's an afterlife, I'll see you there, Teacher." His hand trembled as he held Yeong-hee's letter. His head sank deeply. "Teacher, I'm sorry. It's my fault. Last night, there was no sign of anything wrong, but to say I was thirsty, I went out to buy something to drink, and when I came back late after meeting someone..."

Yeong-hee severed her artery with her 5-month pregnant body. When Sang-ho returned, she was already unconscious, bleeding profusely. He hurriedly called an ambulance. By the time Yeong-hee was diagnosed by the Caucasian doctor, it was too late. She was immediately taken to the morgue. "So, have you contacted Yeong-hee's parents?" "No, Yeong-hee always said things like that. Even if I die, I won't let my parents know. I just brushed it off back then." He slowly got up. Leaving the store to someone else, he headed to the hospital where Yeong-hee was. The white sheet covering her body in the morgue was like a movie scene. He silently kneeled before it, bowing his head. "Yeong-hee, I apologize. Forgive us. It wasn't your fault that you had to go like this. Things will get better from now on. I believe there won't be another child like you." Beside him, Sang-ho whimpered like a child throwing a tantrum. "Yeong-hee, it's because of me that you died." Sang-ho wiped his tears roughly with both fists and pounded the wall. "Let's go, let's go tell Yeong-hee's parents."

When Yeong-hee's father heard the news, he let out a long sigh without saying a word.

Yeong-hee's mother, who was beside him, cried out, "Oh, my child," her voice tearing apart. The pyramid-like stacks of apples and oranges on the store's display shelf seemed to pound like drums, hitting her chest. "Oh, why is this happening! Shameful!" Her husband yelled angrily. He clenched his jaw and harshly slammed the cash register as a customer handed over a bill. Yeong-hee's funeral was attended by Yeong-hee's parents, siblings, and about ten young men and women, conducted modestly under the guidance of a pastor the next day. Hyun looked up at the sky as Yeong-hee's body was covered with earth. The sunlight was warm. Was winter already passing and spring arriving? Over a corner of the cemetery, forsythias bloomed brightly, swaying in the still chilly wind. A few sparrows lined up neatly on the tombstone, hopping on the grass that had just started to grow. Beyond the cemetery, a bridge spanned the highway between leafless branches, shimmering silver in the March sunlight. "Yeong-hee, you're a bridge. A bridge on our path forward. Were you in pain? But behind that pain, countless dreams are rising. I see them."

It felt like Yeong-hee's sunny voice could be heard. It seemed like she was talking while basking in the warm spring sunlight. Looking at the bridge, one might want to cross it at least once, wanting to become that bridge, the one sturdy, beautiful, and lovely bridge we cross. Yeong-hee's mother couldn't stop crying from start to finish, while her father, eyes wide open, remained silent until the end.

Bees Meet Flowers!

It was a Saturday. A week had passed since Yeong-hee's funeral. Ji-ae missed her terribly. Hyun called Ji-ae. Ji-ae, busy cleaning the house, answered after a few 'hellos' as if she had been asleep and finally heard Hyun's voice. "Ji-ae, do you have time?" "Yes, I do." Of course, she did. For him, she would always wait by the roadside, like a winter tree swaying in the wind. He approached her. Under the streetlight's glow, his eyes were quietly boiling. He seemed taller. Without a word, he opened the car door. "Everyone issues their own checks to live on."

As they exited the highway towards Brooklyn, he suddenly spoke. Ji-ae looked at him, puzzled. He didn't look back at Ji-ae. "Ji-ae, I think I've irresponsibly issued my own checks." "Why would you say that...? What happened?" "It's distressing. A young girl committed suicide. You might remember her. We just attended her funeral recently. Her mother couldn't stop crying, and her father remained silent until the end." "I'm sorry. I didn't know about that. Why didn't you call me?" Ji-ae placed her hand on his, which was holding the steering wheel. Her chest tightened. It felt like riding on waves of warmth, hearing the dull sound of a hammer. Following that sound, long-forgotten poetry bubbled up. "I can't make anything joyful for you, but I want to be a precious love for you. Every night, I fall asleep alone, but you hold my hand by my side. Even when I cry in sadness, you're there, smiling at me."

A groan escaped his lips. "Ji-ae, did Yeong-hee take responsibility for her own checks? Oh, I don't know. Nothing's certain. That girl was too young." He parked the car in the highway parking lot, clasping his hands on the steering wheel as if gripping his thoughts. "Hyun, why torment yourself like this? It's too late to question whose responsibility it is. Hyun, you did your best. It's not your fault if things didn't turn out." "Ji-ae, please stop talking. Just leave me alone for a bit." The cars raced along the highway like hungry beasts. The intermittent sound of waves, like the buzzing of bees, accompanied the engine's roar, circling around their ears. "Shall we go out?" he said. They walked in silence. They saw a hill they had been to before. It was surrounded by thin shrubs in the distance. He spread his biker jacket on the ground, creating a hollow space for Ji-ae. They sat facing the sea. The wind, which had been blowing moments ago, died down, and there was no sound of waves anymore.

"Although she ended her own life, her death could serve as a silent resistance, urging society to urgently address the issues facing our youth. Her quiet death could become a catalyst, a stepping stone, as it has always been," he said, compassionately continuing as Ji-ae bowed her head between her knees. "To prevent another tragedy, a greater tragedy, and to receive the turn of good deeds from it. People or events become fertilizer, flowers bloom upon them, mountain ranges rise, and thus humanity continues to live unchanged, isn't it?" Suddenly, Hyun looked up at Ji-ae. "Are you still writing poetry?" "No, it's been a long time since I've done that. Since I came to the United States." "Why? Did life here make it so difficult for Ji-ae?" "No, it's not that. I feel like you cling too tightly to yourself, even more than I do. It seems too difficult for you. Of course, your dedication to those kids seems noble, but..." "You flatter me! But more than that, I feel like I've been living too long in a monologue. Sometimes, not seizing the opportunity when I know there's another path, not grabbing it, feels like my own arrogance and selfishness."

A few strands of Ji-ae's hair fluttered in the wind, covering her forehead slightly. "Living in the United States, I feel like my nerves are gradually dulling, unknowingly. Sometimes, it's relieving, but it's painful." His eyes were fixed on the horizon, where the boundary was blurred by the fog. Ji-ae's gaze followed him towards the darkening end of the sea. Suddenly, her heart fluttered. She buried her head between her knees. Suddenly, she smelled pine trees. It was the scent of pine mixed with the scent of spring breeze through wildflowers. She saw herself rushing into the depths of the scent. Mind and body. The fragrance emanated from him. He put his arm around Ji-ae's shoulder and embraced her. A breeze blew from somewhere. The color of the sea leaned towards mist, and the sea began to move quietly with strokes of indigo and white. Was it the wind blowing from the sea? The sea roared towards them. Hyun buried his face. His body trembled as he pressed against her chest. "I endured it. Compared to living without news for twenty years, it's nothing," he muttered to himself. "But not being able to meet you when you're right in front of me was even more unbearable." His voice sounded like the last tantrum of a tired child. A bird chirped softly from Ji-ae's throat. Ready to fly, I'll try to fly too.

"I will try to fly in that blue sky," the bird chirped louder. Her throat felt hot. Hyun buried his head in her chest and then lifted it up again. Four moist eyes were close by. Ji-ae felt a faint sun between them and lowered her eyes. "I thought of Ji-ae while facing death in Vietnam. Looking back now, it feels like my dedication to Ji-ae has held me together until today." His words soaked Ji-ae entirely. They led her underwater. Only the sound of the waves, not the seagulls' cries, was heard. The waves brought him to the door. Opening the door, he roughly led the woman inside. Deep into the most beautiful mountains, a painful fireworks display burst, binding their bodies together. How much time had passed? The sound of car tires on the highway crackled. He held Ji-ae tightly and wept. She felt a moment of shame as a woman. Then something white fell from the sky. They were small things; it was snowing late in spring. Ji-ae spent that night holding the collapsed embankment of the reservoir. The scolding that pierced like thorns plagued her existence, stirring chaos deep within her, tangling every thread of consciousness.

"Ji-ae, live kindly. A woman should keep herself presentable wherever she goes." Did Mom say she would teach her children even after death? Somewhere in her consciousness, she was being reprimanded. 'Mom, he's openly living with a hometown woman in Korea... Now I'll open the door. I'm too stifled. I feel like I can't breathe. I'm not Mom. I'm not Mom.' So she suffered for days. As the sediment of pain and confusion settled, a gradual transformation occurred within her. Like a tender shoot pushing through gravel.

Every cell seemed to gain vigor, as if intoxicated by a fragrant brew, spreading its wings. It was an emergency of pain. After the agony passed, Ji-ae found tranquility in the deeper depths of her inner self. In the depth of tranquility, Hyun smiled. With a brighter face, with thicker and stronger ties, was it happiness? Was it a medicine that healed my soul? He was like a fish leaping in Ji-ae's sea. Soaring high with the wave crest, then descending deep into the abyss along with the waves. There was trust. Is complete trust in one person so wonderful? She saw the sprout of faith blooming there. Is God trying to prove His love to humanity through that seed?

For that, did he become a human descending into the creation of the window he made? Ji-ae accepted the trust in that love through Hyeon. But Ji-ae still can't help but wander why. Thinking of Hyeon, the faces of her husband and son alternately come to mind, and the endless clues constantly revolve, bringing moments of relaxation and tension, pain and joy. Ah, when will my suffering, the torment of my existence, come to an end? During the harvest thanksgiving, her son came home for a while. "Mother, here he is." With a smile on his face, her son introduced his fiancée standing beside him. Jane shyly nodded in greeting. "Welcome! I've heard a lot about you." As she reached out her hand, there was a strange tremor in her chest. Our blue-eyed grandson, our third generation. Suddenly, that thought came to her. It was going on smoothly. It was never a feeling she disliked. Ji-ae sat them down and brewed tea. She poured the boiling water slowly into cups. Strangely, her husband's face came to mind in the steam rising from the cup. It was a face she had long forgotten. Your son is marrying a blue-eyed...

Meeting the wife. Ji-ae felt a faint contradiction. When her son first mentioned his marriage to Jane over the phone, she felt strong resistance. Why does it have to be an American, why not someone born and raised here with two-year-olds? But since she knew well about Jane through her son, she congratulated her son. "Mom, she's just like a Korean kid. No, she's more Korean than other Korean kids born and raised here. She was born and raised in Korea. Her parents run an educational business in Korea, and Jane only came here to study at university." And her son added, "I've learned a lot about

Korea from my friends. Of course, I've learned a lot of Korean too."
Jane kept smiling. "Mom, I told you on the phone, but I came here
to get your permission." Her son became serious, not patting his
fiancée's shoulders. And after looking at his mother's face for a while,
he said, "Mom, it's weird. You're weird." "What's weird?" "Well, it's
weird. There's something different about you. Mom, you seem happy
without harvesting laughter from your son, staring at her with a curi-
ous face."

"What's odd? No, are you happy?" "Mom, you've changed. I
sense a completely different atmosphere. You've definitely changed.
There's a different scent in the air. I can't quite put my finger on
it." Ji-ae felt strange hearing her son's words. Changed, no, are you
happy? Are you asking me if I'm happy? But she turned her face
without saying a word and changed the subject. "But have you set
the date?" "Yes, we decided on Christmas Eve." Suddenly, Ji-ae's eyes
widened. It felt like centuries had passed since the college president of
the small Midwestern town in the United States where they attended
university had paired the lonely and tired pair of Korean exchange
students. "Mom, what's wrong?" "Are you feeling unwell?" The two
young people looked at her alternately, concerned. "No, nothing. It's
nothing." She shook her head. "Jaesik, after your wedding, I'll return
to our homeland for a while." "What?" "I said I'm going back to our
homeland." She repeated the words she hadn't expected to say. Yes, I
will go too.

I'll go and confess everything to my husband and gain my free-
dom. Forgiveness and freedom. Whatever he did to me, it's not my
problem. I'll seek forgiveness from him, and we must reconcile. Yes,
reconciliation. True human happiness starts from reaching out to
each other, holding hands, and supporting each other. It transcends
understanding. I'll extend my hand to him first, grant him the free-
dom he desires, and gain my own freedom too. Fortunately, my son
didn't ask why I was going. "Mom, you've been away for too long."
"Yes, you're right. I've been away too long. That place isn't my coun-
try, is it?" "You're not planning to stay permanently, are you?" "No, of
course not. I'm just visiting for a while." Jane, who had been listening
quietly, interjected. "I truly admire your decision, Mom. I believe

you'll be even happier when you return. Of course, you'll come back soon." "Thank you, Jane." "I think people who leave their hometowns are unhappy. Do they find true freedom and happiness?" Yes, I must reconcile with my homeland too. My mother is no longer here, and I don't know where my relatives are, but my friends are scattered all over, and I don't know where they live.

Touching and tasting the soil and wind of one's homeland, seeing the changed face of one's homeland with one's own eyes. Oh, how wonderful it would be. My stifled heart would surely burst open. Ji-ae carefully examined Jane's face again. The round face, the slightly downturned nose, the doll-like innocent eyes, and the thin lips seemed both innocent and intelligent. "And Mom, I shouldn't say this, but it seems like Koreans know so little about their own country. It's truly a beautiful country." Jane blushed and lowered her head. Ji-ae looked at Jane with admiration in her eyes. Ah, I see. Worrying about your relationship was a futile gesture. "Culture is in the heart, not in the skin. It's in the mind." Ji-ae remembered Hyun's words about knowledge and relationships. Are his words right? She wondered. Ji-ae filled the glasses with water. "For your marriage." "Thank you, Mom." "Thank you too." Clink, the glasses touched each other. "And for your return, Mom."

Jane raised her glass even higher and shouted with a droplet-like voice, "Thank you." However, she felt a certain unease amidst the excitement the two young people were giving her. An inexplicable fear crept into her heart. "Mom, I know. A person's worth is not in their skin. We live in a time where individuals are evaluated based on their worth and abilities. Moreover, I believe America is like that." Through the silence, her son's excited voice was heard piercing through. 'Yes, you once asked. What does it mean to become Korean? Now you seem to know. You gained it through Jane, and you're happy. Thank you, my son. Yes, the wilderness is satisfied with one generation. It's been a long time since we entered the era of being evaluated based on ability, so why did your dad insist on returning to our homeland so stubbornly? He's wandering like a rootless tree. Why is that? Ah, does he have a place to settle? Is it his hometown in the North? Hyun said, the homeland is in the heart and mind. But he has suffered too much. Refusing to heal, he's suffering. I wept at the Tower of Freedom. I cried out in the empty place. The lamentation at the Tower of Freedom. After his boiling lament, I hope he finds new roots deep down and blossoms with new fruits, to be happy.'

Mi-young's Departure
and Hyun's Accident

"Ji-ae," Mi-young announced as she entered, stirring the air. "I just happened to be passing by." "Ah, good to see you. When are you leaving?" "This week will be my last." "What will I do without you?" Ji-ae has been sorrowful about Mi-young's transfer since she heard about it a month ago. "I still can't understand your change of heart. Why aren't you staying here?" "Well, I just wanted to change my environment," Mi-young replied, her gaze unexpectedly calm. "I need to go now. I'm busy." She turned and walked away like a stranger. When did Mi-young start treating me this way? It's always been pleasant when we meet.

Mi-young's cheerful demeanor had turned as stiff as tree bark, starting to make their relationship awkward. It began around the time when Ji-ae and Hyun had that incident at the beach. Mi-young was such a sharp girl, always quick to notice things between us. Ji-ae felt awkward dealing with her friend as Mi-young's attitude suddenly changed and she decided to leave. Ji-ae stared at Mi-young's back. Mi-young, forgive me. We couldn't help it. A week later, Mi-young parked her car, loaded with luggage, and stepped out. "Could you at least say goodbye to Hyun before you go?" "No, you can do that for me. Tell him I couldn't see him before leaving." Mi-young spoke calmly and glanced at Ji-ae before continuing. "Ji-ae, he's truly a great person. I sincerely hope you and him will be happy." "How can you say that! I'm not sure of anything." "This young one, happiness isn't something anyone can easily attain. You and Hyun can be enough for each other. And happiness doesn't come whenever you want it, its footsteps are swift." Ji-ae choked up. She held her leaving friend's hand and hugged her tightly.

"How will I manage without you? I feel so empty," she said. "Still such a girl, even as you grow older... you still have a long way to go," Mi-young laughed. Ji-ae sensed something strange in that laughter, something different than before. "Ji-ae, remember this: It is our utmost duty to be happy," Mi-young said with a fleeting melancholy that quickly gave way to a warm breeze, like fragrance. Ah, that was it—the change Ji-ae had felt earlier. It was a change she had never seen or felt in Mi-young before. The solitude on her face faded quickly, replaced by a bright smile. Ji-ae found an unexpected comfort in Mi-young's laughter and looked at her thoughtfully. "I've really enjoyed being with you... I'm sorry." "Why? What for?" Mi-young quickly opened the car door and slid inside. "I'll get in touch," she said curtly, starting the engine. She handed Ji-ae a note with the same smile as before, not looking back as she drove away. Standing there, Ji-ae unfolded the note from Mi-young. "Ji-ae, I went back there last night. I wanted to let everything go, just like them. Tears flowed."

Tears she hadn't shed for a long time. And that person is coming back. How infinitely warm that person is to my empty heart! And freedom, it was so easy. Was there such a deep root of human dignity beyond my consciousness, filled with thorns... That's the freedom, the happiness I want to share with you! After Yeong-hee's funeral, rumors spread that Sang-ho had disappeared into a Chinese gang the next day. On Saturday evening, Hyun closed the shop early and went to Chinatown. The place where Sang-ho was said to be located was a narrow alley lined with Chinese restaurants on both sides. How far did he walk in? Suddenly, Hyun felt a sharp pain in his side and collapsed. Feeling someone rifling through his pockets, he lost consciousness. "Teacher..." Sang-ho's urgent voice faintly pierced through his senses, the distant sound of an ambulance... Hyun regained consciousness late at night in the hospital. Sang-ho was kneeling by the bedside, crying. With Ji-ae sitting with a worried look against the white wall. "Ah, you're awake," Ji-ae exclaimed, startled. Looking at her, a faint smile crept onto Hyun's pale face.

The surgeon who operated on Hyun remarked that it was fortunate the knife had missed vital areas, although there was significant bleeding and the wounds were deep. Hyun would need to be hospitalized and on an IV for at least fifteen days. The doctor added, "It could have been a serious situation if the knife had gone slightly deeper. It seems your God was looking out for you." During Hyun's hospitalization, Sang-ho visited daily. He apologized to his father and took over running the store in Hyun's place while staying at home. Other children who had run away with Sang-ho also returned home and went back to school. Sang-ho managed the store during the day with the help of a waitress and attended night school to finish his remaining courses. He planned to enter the city university next year to major in business administration. Ji-ae, after finishing work, would visit Hyun. When he was discharged and confined to a wheelchair, she frequently traveled to his home to take care of him. A month after Hyun's discharge, on a Saturday, as Ji-ae was arranging the vegetables she had brought, Hyun said, "You've worked so hard. Thank you." There was a deep, uncharacteristic shadow in his eyes as he looked at Ji-ae, a change from before. Ji-ae shifted her gaze from him to his long, thick, pale fingers neatly resting outside the boldly striped orange and blue blanket. Their eyes interlocked momentarily. Ji-ae, avoiding his gaze, looked toward the white wall.

A month had passed since Hyun's discharge from the hospital. Ji-ae set aside the vegetables she had brought and sat facing him. Hyun said, "You've worked too hard all this time. Thank you." There was a deep shadow in his eyes as he gently met Ji-ae's gaze. Ji-ae glanced at his hands, neatly arranging the thin, blue-striped blanket with his pale, thick fingers. Their eyes met. Even without looking at him, Ji-ae could feel the meaning behind his gaze. "Ji-ae, you don't have to come anymore. I have Sang-ho now. I can move on my own too." Seeing Ji-ae's hesitant gaze, he lowered his eyes. "You've done so much for me. Thank you!" He sighed, as if exhaling heavily. "..." "I'll contact you soon." It had been over a month since their last meeting with Hyun, and he hadn't called once. Ji-ae hadn't called either. Yet she waited. Didn't he say he would contact her? One day, over a month later, Hyun hurried out to go to the consulate. He walked out with a cane instead of crutches. The cold wind outside the door chilled his hands as he paused to write his repatriation application. His eyes flickered with pain. Ji-ae, leaving you behind! But you'll understand, won't you?

Ji-ae returned from work and opened the mailbox. Hyun's letter was nestled among the advertisements and magazines. Her hands trembled as she tore open the letter. Ji-ae, by the time you hold this letter, I will have already left this place and gone. I am returning to our homeland. Please forgive me. I believe you will understand this decision of mine to leave silently. I didn't think this way at first. But I came to believe that this was the only way to make us stronger. Ji-ae, even if we abandon our homeland, our homeland will never abandon us. Our homeland is always open like a mother's embrace. I believe that. Right now, our homeland is tied with iron chains around its waist, but someday, trust and love will bloom from the 38th parallel line. Didn't I say that someday? That one cannot compete fully with a whole person using only one leg. This is our reality. But someday in the near future, our wounds will heal. Miracles will happen. That's why I decided not to turn away. I have seen wandering youths more than anything while reading newspapers from the homeland. They are the precious future wounded by the excessive greed and indifference of adults. I couldn't turn away from that burden. I decided to do my small part...

We will prevail. The time is already here when we, who have gone forward with one leg while others have both legs, will show our prowess even in the game of those with two legs before the time comes. Ji-ae, don't be upset that I'm leaving. We are always together. There is no farewell for us anymore. I have experienced the tremendous grace that the two of us can be happy together now. That grace gave me the strength to make this decision. I knew Ji-ae's unspoken worries. I almost felt like I knew why Mr. Park Jae-hoon stayed in Korea for so long without divorcing Ji-ae. Time will solve everything. But we can't build a house on someone else's grave, can we? In a postscript, he added, "I've entrusted the store to the manager, so go there occasionally and give him some encouragement." Ji-ae clenched the letter and sat down as if she might collapse onto the chair.

Ah, Freedom!

She hummed softly. Plop, plop. Among the branches outside the window, sparrows chirped as she stood up with the letter in her hand, looking out the window. The morning sun created a bluish-gray satin thread, and faint mist-like substance covered it. Something hot welled up in her throat. She felt parched and burnt. Strength drained from her body. She gripped the window sill. Ji-ae, my wandering is over. With your help, Ji-ae. Returning to our homeland means meeting you, who is in the pain of our land and in those clouds in the sky, together. Even if we abandon our homeland, our homeland hasn't abandoned us. Our homeland is always open like a mother's embrace. Oh, Hyun, what are you? You speak of the happiness of two people.

Suddenly, Ji-ae felt like she was an orphan of heaven. No tears came out. Oh, Hyun, what are you trying to prove? You said I would understand. Ji-ae sighed. But Ji-ae seemed to understand Hyun's intention. Why she wandered for so long. Ah, was it because she left her homeland? Like old clothes that have clung to the body comfortably for a long time, is her loneliness that follows her like her own flesh because she left the embrace of her motherland? But, but, nothing was transparent to her now. From the healed wound of her injury, pus oozed out, and broken branches just swayed in the storm. Ji-ae habitually recited the third day Helen Keller spoke of in 'If I Could See You for Three Days': "I will wake up in the morning when the east is red, I will see the busy people going to work, the movement of cars rushing like spider webs, I will go to the theater and listen to the actors' performances and the songs of opera singers, and at night, I will look at the high-rise buildings buried in neon signs and the many products displayed in the show windows, and then I will return home. Spending time like this, when my eyes close again into eternal darkness, I will quietly thank my God for three days of precious experiences and opportunities."

When everything in daily life becomes opaque, when living feels tired, weary, and dull, when I wish I could just disappear from this world and sleep, every time, Helen Keller's simple gratitude confession, which she sucked like a mother's nipple. Memorizing that forgotten confession, she reproached herself. Hundreds of times, thousands of times given three days. Haven't I had the blessing of those three days she wished for all my life? Living life complaining and forgetting gratitude for the life I've been given shamefully struck her most tender conscience. I have too much overflowing. Dostoevsky's five minutes of longing also crossed her mind. If I were given the last five minutes? The light that reflected the bones of death Hyun experienced in Vietnam, what did Mi-young mean when she said she wanted to share with you? Ji-ae stayed awake all night and fell asleep in the early morning hours. It was a dream. In her dream, she was climbing a hill with faint light. Grasping the dry weeds and sweating profusely, she climbed. The bright face of little Jack, who smiled sunnily even though he died recently, Mrs. Kim, who diligently raises her son while being abused by her husband, still cheerful Julie in the children's ward, the bright smiling face of Mi-young, the determined face of Hyun, the dark and desperate look of Park Jaehoon, the hopeful eyes of a son, my own bright blue eyes, faces of various skin colors in hospitals, an old man sitting on a wheelchair and his faithful companion, pedestrians overflowing on the street,

In the basement and in the alley, street musicians raised their voices in song, their instruments clashing melodically against the crisp music of the coast guard's brass. The young people at Hyun's coffee shop, and Young-hee... At first, their faces were like small dots, forming a circle that gradually grew larger and wider. Over time, it became a vast, timeless circle that expanded even further, spreading out into the distance... A single blade of grass, assuming the visage of a human, lifted its head in the wind, and gradually, more blades arose, layer by layer, becoming faces that laughed and danced—a multitude of colorful flowers. From nowhere, butterflies converged—silver, gold, and tiger butterflies mingling in a flutter of colors, their delicate wings creating the sound of a celestial choir. She collapsed to her knees beneath the window. In a dream within a dream, she saw herself as such, a hand reaching out to her. From long ago, the monstrous figures that haunted her consciousness still roamed, their chains of emptiness and despair heavy. They eagerly engaged in deceit, stirring up a whirlwind to cover the hand reaching out, attempting to flee. The hand reaching towards her was relentless, as if bloodied and crowned with thorns, with nails crudely hammered in. In some street, any street, faces that one might pass without a second thought—dirty, discarded like piles of garbage, emanating foul odors, the kind of faces she had seen often yet never dared to confront directly—now, that person was whispering softly to her.

Ji-ae, do you know what love is? Do you realize that I have devoted my all to create you with celestial beauty? I already see your perfect completion. It suddenly became clear to me. My entire body felt as if it were being heated by a fierce bonfire. My previously stifled chest bloomed open like a flower in spring. My heavy shoulders collapsed and flowed away like a river. It was as bright as broad daylight in my dream. What could this be, what could this be? In a drowsy state of consciousness, within another dream layer, the heavy iron masses I had been carrying, the suffocating heaviness, suddenly collapsed. That monstrous thing vanished. Was it grinding its teeth as it fled? That thing which had been ceaselessly manipulated deep within her consciousness. Then, a light pierced her body from head to toe, a light sharp as a knife blade descending to the basement's depths, coursing through her core like an electric current.

It was fleeting. A ray of light descended from some corner beyond the universe faster and clearer than a shooting star. It was ah, a fragrance! That fragrance was imprinted in the midst of her existence as a scar of light. Tears flowed uncontrollably. In the dream, tears that couldn't be shed when she was alive, as if the doors of the warehouse of tears, waiting at every place her name was, every step she took, trapped tears had finally met their time, opened the door, and flowed down the cheeks. In the dream, in vivid dreams as if it were daytime. Those tears gave her the freedom of existence! Who am I? That lingering question, just passing by uncertainly, seemed to roll out like a seed bursting from a ripe apricot fruit. The freedom of existence burst out. There, the pain of Hyun's absence, the long-standing frustration towards her husband, the betrayal towards her father, the longing for her mother, the wounds she had received throughout her life, and the guilt, all the things entangling her, were washed away as cleanly as a rite of passage. In the dream, and ah, peace was warm. Bright as dewdrops on the grass leaves, morning was coming with the beauty of freedom.

She lay in bed, reflecting on the dream she had just before falling asleep. With both hands on her chest, she lay there for a while. She savored the dream. Birds were singing. Nature seemed to follow the chirping of the birds as if their existence was irresistibly delightful, and the three realms were opening the door that had been closed.

Beautiful Youths

Sangho was busy bustling around the shop entertaining guests. The waitress who was there before was nowhere to be seen, and about six young people were helping him. Their expressions were consistently bright. Confidence overflowed from their bodies. There was even a girl who was agile like a swallow, someone I hadn't seen before. They were as fresh and lively as the leaves of May. "We've all returned to school. We take turns taking care of the shop," Sangho said, his voice as fresh as the June breeze rippling through pumpkin leaves, delivering news Ji-ae already knew. Then the girl who introduced herself as not herself but another said, "Do you know? We're trying to create a small youth group. The name is not decided yet. Sangho wants to call it 'Yeong-hee's Legs,' but that's too sentimental, so we're thinking of a more solid name." Ah, are they Hyun's incarnations? Even without him, his dream is blooming and growing with them.

He accomplished the task as casually as searching for water when thirsty and food when hungry, without flaunting his name. He offered a life compass to the descendants of Dangun, abandoned on the streets of orphaned children, on these unfamiliar streets of New York. That fire is silently burning in the hearts of these youths. That fire will continue to spread from generation to generation. Hyun, now wandering the streets of his homeland, returned to find wandering youths. He was endlessly proud. "Sangho, shall we close the shop tomorrow and visit the Metropolitan Museum?" Ji-ae said something she hadn't even thought of, looking at them. She felt sorry for them, working diligently without a day off. She wanted to do something for them. After looking at each other for a moment, they clapped their hands together and exclaimed, "Whoo-hoo!" The steps of the Metropolitan Museum, standing tall next to Central Park, were crowded with visitors from around the world. Sangho was busy taking pictures with the camera he brought. Ji-ae, seeing that the children touring the Asian section seemed uninterested, left the museum and went to a Korean restaurant near Broadway at 32nd Street for a meal before going up to the Empire State Building. The children laughed, saying that people walking the streets of New York looked like ants from the top of the building.

That's right. Kids, do you know how small we are? But having dreams makes a difference. Having big dreams can even move mountains," Ji-ae said, to which Sangho replied, "That's correct. Yes, Teacher." They laughed and chatted, finding something amusing. They enjoyed the natural scenery in Central Park, went to a roadside diner for a simple dinner, and parted ways. It was a meaningful day. Ji-ae thought of Hyun as she spent a joyful time with them. She felt happy and content as she rode the subway alone back to Flushing. Ah, this is life, she thought, and this is what happiness feels like.

Park Jae-hoon's Death

At the end of the year, on her way home from the empty office, Ji-ae bought a Korean newspaper published here. When she got home, she quickly showered and picked up the newspaper. As her eyes scanned the headlines on the front page of the society section, they suddenly stopped. "...?? Dr. Park Jae-hoon, an elite scholar studying in the U.S. Found dead under mysterious circumstances near the Han River in the DMZ. Was it suicide, or an accident?" Along with this long headline, there was a picture of him when he was alive. She widened her eyes and leaned closer to the newspaper. The picture depicted a scene of desolation on the steep bank of the dry river and his sad face wandering aimlessly, speaking volumes. His body seemed scattered like shattered pieces among the small, excavated circles among the thickets. "He was found in the northernmost area of the Han River, the cause of death unknown..."

She couldn't read any further. Putting down the newspaper, she held her head in her hands and closed her eyes. Oh no, this couldn't be happening! "His mother, alone, looks at the southern sky every day and clasps her hands to her chest... Some say he was traveling back and forth along the Han River..." His lament, without any coherence, struck her mind. Wasn't his letter from a month ago saying it? That he saw the unified future of our homeland while his mother looked north from the Tower of Freedom? But now, he's gone like this! He used to explore Ji-ae's thoughts about going north after receiving his degree. Has he gone back to the hometown he used to dream of... The newspaper was too simplistic. Why did he go alone to the northernmost region where civilians rarely ventured... Wasn't it the most intense part of the Central Front during the Korean War? Wasn't it where many refugees seeking freedom from the south were indiscriminately shot? Authorities simply said he seemed to have stepped on a landmine. Ji-ae felt like she understood the meaning of his death. The anxiety and fear he must have endured alone in such a troubled and difficult time, leaving his family behind. His pride couldn't tolerate those feelings. Like a snail, struggling in the dark of loneliness and resentment...

Did he resist the sad and unjust history by choosing death? No. Didn't he speak of a new life? Wasn't he filled with hope for reunification? Did he, missing his mother and following the riverbank where he used to come down from the north, stumble as authorities said? He is an atonement of history. No, not just that. Many people shed blood like sand in the long pages of history! With difficulty obtaining permission from the authorities, his funeral was planned to be held modestly with professors, students who had taught him, and a few relatives on a hill overlooking the Han River. It was the northernmost area accessible to civilians. His homeland he couldn't return to alive. She wanted to lay him to rest closer to home, even just a little bit. It was a heart of atonement. As the workers dug the grave, Ji-ae came out alone and looked at the northern sky. The northern sky was all blood-red. A terminal pain seemed to emanate from the crimson light draped over the hill like a writhing dragon. It felt like she was witnessing the agonizing pain of a woman emerging from that light. "How can a person with one leg endure being pushed around? Freedom, freedom... The people starving for freedom like us..." Hyun's words, and the words of the old man she met on a flight to the United States twenty years ago, came to mind without warning.

The dying child carried on her back, the Vietnamese woman risking her life to break through enemy lines. The young Vietnamese man who plunged into the Mekong River with a patriotic poem. Wasn't it all done in the name of the homeland? The invisible bridge of freedom hidden beneath the trees in the northern sky. A place where not even a single ant could pass without permission. Next to it lies a rusted iron bridge, a silent symbol of the screams of bloodshed and the forced silence of compatriots. Waiting eagerly for the last train, the echoes of parents and siblings tearing their chests apart as they lament for their lost loved ones still resonate near the Imjin River. "⊠, why must the ground freeze like this..." The complaint of a worker struggling with his shovel was heard. A chilly wind blew once again. Ji-ae adjusted her black scarf covering her head. The clouds had now dispersed, and as the ashes began to scatter around, a sense of unease lingered. A few pheasants flew across the riverbank, disappearing into the forest on the other side. The sky now began to be tinged with golden and azure-gray hues. Does death make people more generous? Tears slowly flowed down her cheeks. Tears that she didn't shed even at her father's funeral.

The cold winter wind rustled the branches around her. The funeral rites began. Then, from behind her, came the sobbing of a woman. Soon, her sobbing turned into wailing. "No, no, this can't be happening!" What was the woman refusing? Her refusal, mixed with the desperate cries of anguish bursting from her soul! Ji-ae turned her head towards the source of the sound. There, a neat woman in a black coat with a black scarf, whose presence she hadn't noticed before, was digging the ground with gloved hands, crying uncontrollably. Ah, it all made sense now! The woman who had traveled from the north to wait for him alone. The pain that time had inflicted upon her surged in Ji-ae's chest. A mound was raised. A mirage shimmered in Ji-ae's eyes on the small grassy mound of the mound. It was a butterfly. A single butterfly extended its wings as if about to take flight, and in an instant, countless butterflies fluttered into the air. His colleagues erected a small wooden plaque labeled 'Park Jae-hoon's Tomb'. That's when it happened. Ji-ae was drawn by a powerful force to look up. "Ah, Hyun!" Leaning against a sycamore tree on the other side, Hyun stood with a cane in one hand, facing her.

He was slowly making his way towards her, leaning lightly on his cane. She didn't move until he got closer. "Thank you for everything." She bowed her head. Her legs trembled. "I'll go. There's a car waiting." He reached out his hand, not holding the cane, and guided her arm. "No, I'm fine." Ji-ae turned her head and slowly descended the hill, leaving him behind. The woman was nowhere to be seen. She turned to look at the northern sky again. Holding Hyun's dark silhouette in her heart, the place, now covered with a hazy twilight without clouds, was peaceful. The peace she saw with Hyun over the Atlantic Ocean in New York seemed to resonate in the chirping of the birds, as if the unified chorus of the north and south praising the reunified homeland. It was neither a hallucination nor an auditory illusion, Ji-ae shook her head.

Meeting Again!

Six months had swiftly passed. After receiving the news of working for a youth rehabilitation center in Daejeon, their time had passed uneventfully. On that Friday, Ji-ae walked along the path through the grove of trees towards the main square, unlike her usual routine. The early summer evening sun was casting a warm glow beyond the Momus building. As she approached the entrance of the hospital, she lifted her head as if drawn by something. Ah, there was a familiar face! A tall man emerged from the thicket of trees, his eager gaze enveloping Ji-ae's entire body. 'Ah, Hyun.' Ji-ae saw herself running towards him without hesitation, as if driven by a gust of wind. She embraced Hyun tightly. Oh, how? How was this possible? Shoulders shook with sobs. Nestled in his embrace, she buried her face in his chest. He cupped her face with both hands as if holding a vessel filled with water. Tears mingled from their eyes, wetting each other's skin.

I couldn't bear it. I wanted to see you!" "Me too, me too!" He silenced her with a kiss, his lips warm. Ji-ae turned away from the still deeply sleeping Hyun and stood by the window, gazing at the forest of Central Park. With a week left in August, the morning light, tinged with the hues of early autumn, painted the canopy of the forest in rainbow colors. Soon, the morning sun rose. As if adorning the forest's canopy with golden threads... Ji-ae was dazzled. Along with the sunlight, the fragrance of ripe peaches flowed down her throat. Through Hyun, Ji-ae learned that sex was pain. It was about one person, with a cold and arrogant presence, painfully tearing and widening the deepest part of another human being. It was about being able to pour the springwater of one's soul into that place. Sex was a prayer for reconciliation with the world, for rest. "O my dove, in the clefts of the rock, in the hiding places on the mountainside, show me your face, let me hear your voice; for your voice is sweet, and your face is lovely. You have stolen my heart, my sister, my bride; you have stolen my heart with one glance of your eyes, with one jewel of your necklace." Indeed.

North wind, rise. South wind, come. Blowing in my garden, sending fragrance, the soul and body at the apex of current love spread their wings to the fullest. At that moment, quietly from his lips flowed Solomon's Song of Songs. "Thank you, thank you for coming, thank you, thank you!" Ji-ae got a vacation for Hyun and spent a primitive week in Montauk, at the southern tip of Long Island, New York, with the sound of waves crashing and the sand of the beach. That week was too short. The struggling sound of waves and countless stars of the sky pouring down like brilliant dances, a perpetual festival of heaven and sea... There, time also hid its traces. Why did he only take a week off? Leaving behind regret, at the airport, Ji-ae didn't leave, but a mutual friend saw him off instead. She wanted to hold him in her body forever. There is no parting with him! But she knew. Someday, even this would pass. Listening to the waves of Montauk, she thought. Just like the waves hitting and licking the rocks and sand of the beach, everything would disappear one day.

Hyun's KAL 007 Disaster

The day after Hyun left, the hospital was unusually noisy. People gathered in the downstairs lounge with a TV screen. On the screen, urgent news from a feverish announcer was being broadcast. "Korean Air Lines Flight 007, which penetrated deep into Soviet territory after a long pursuit by Soviet aircraft..." As the announcer finished speaking, a virtual airplane in the air burst into fireworks and disappeared. Then came the demonstration of Koreans holding the UN flag. Detailed explanations from the announcer followed. "Yesterday, Korean Air Lines Flight 007, a Boeing 747 en route from Kennedy Airport to Seoul, was shot down by Soviet fighter missiles over the waters near Sakhalin, causing the deaths of all 269 crew members and passengers from various countries worldwide." The intense and poignant report from the announcer continued.

Ji-ae immediately went up to the office and called the Korean Air New York office. His hands trembled like leaves in the wind. He mentioned his name. Did he happen to be among the passengers who departed yesterday? He mentioned his name. "Yes, Mr. Jinhyun, he was among the passengers... It's certain. But with him?" The receiver dropped. From within the receiver, Ji-ae faintly heard the last words, like a distant tape being cut off abruptly. The next thing Ji-ae knew, he was back in the hospital bed. How much time had passed, how many months or years? Time seemed uncertainly frozen in a remote uninhabited island in the middle of the sea, where the rise and fall of nations were vague. Mi-young's worried face was faintly visible right beside the bed. Everything was white, pure white. The walls of the hospital room, the curtains, Mi-young... Above them, a thin layer of ice seemed to have melted, and a faint storm cloud floated hazily. "Are you feeling better now?" Mi-young's voice sounded faint. "I...

decided to come back. We'll work together again..." It seemed like she heard such words again. "You stubborn thing, cheer up!" She held Ji-ae's wrist with a pale smile. Her hand was very warm. Ji-ae received a few more drips, rested for a few days, and got up again.

Mi-young took care of everything after Hyun's passing. The compensation for his service was donated to the Daejeon Youth Rehabilitation Center, where he had briefly worked. A building and a playground were expanded in his name, and at the entrance, a monument bearing his name was erected with the inscription: "Greater love hath no one than this, that one lay down his life for his friends." Today, as on many days, Ji-ae takes her break by the window, gazing outside. Winter has passed, and the forsythia bushes are trembling in the wind with clusters of yellow blossoms. The sunlight was bright and cheerful. An elderly couple passes by; one seated in a wheelchair, the other pushing it. They exchange laughs and tender words, as if all the time in the world were made for them alone. Ah, Hyun! His departure feels like something out of a fairy tale. No, it seems unbelievable. Ji-ae shakes her head. 'He is gone. He burned brightly in his short life. He may be gone, but the sparks he left continue to grow. They will burn on, as long as the earth endures, in the lives of women and men, in the hearts of young people across the sea who wander not knowing their path, it will spread across the world. Like air, like wind—with wings.' Ji-ae looks down the bush-lined path. Beyond the traffic and the towering buildings, it's as if Hyun is there, still smiling.

As a sliver of sunlight expanded, it took the shape of a large bird, fluttering its wings like a butterfly. Her eyes moistened. Since he had left, the seasons had changed twice, and even as the third season arrived, nothing had changed for her.

The Darkness Lifts

The light clings to the brow of dawn after a long night, in a land where there is no sadness, pain, or inequality—the land of the sun. The eastern sun was within us, growing in our sinews and blood, even amidst pain, misunderstanding, and absurdity. The tireless peace efforts of domestic and international civilian organizations, the recent landmark agreement between the President of South Korea and the UN Secretary-General, and notably, the solo demonstration by Korean-American teenager Lee Seong-min at Beijing's Tiananmen Square, have captured global attention and cultivated a mood conducive to the long-desired unification of the 80 million people of the nation.

Along the Han River, the Arirang Peace Farm and the World Children's Peace Park have been established. Today, the opening ceremony of the World Peace Youth Arirang Cultural Center is marked by a joint concert featuring North and South Korean musicians, with the attendance of dignitaries from various countries and an excited audience of all ages, including children. As winter deepens, the longing for spring intensifies—let the sounds of peace and freedom ring powerfully through the 5,000-year-old history of the Korean vine. Let it spread brilliantly. Ah, unification, unification across the three thousand ri of beautiful Korea! Rise, rise, oh sun! Spread across the whole world! Accompanied by the orchestral accompaniment, the peaceful chorus of the mass choir flowed like a gentle river across the plains. Ji-ae, as if awakening from a deep sleep or returning from a lengthy reverie, was brought back to the present. The applause from the audience, as vigorous as the rustling of plants across the three thousand ri, seemed unending.

Without a trace of emotion, even in the face of her grandmother sitting beside her, deeply moved, she looked up at the sky. The sky over the DMZ, free from pollution, was endlessly clear and blue. The fragrant breeze of May was delightful. Ji-ae signaled with her eyes for Ji-han to stand up, then gently took his wrist and rose quietly. The peculiar trees and flowers sent from various countries surrounding the building emitted a subtle fragrance. It was peaceful. Right here, right now, there was a promise for tomorrow, hope, and trust. The whole world is united for the equality of humanity and the beautiful life of you and me. Not a word about nuclear weapons. Right here, right now, the sinister and ignorant face of nuclear weapons was not visible. Ji-ae wanted to believe in that moment. Yes, we must believe. We must move forward for that. The long tragedy of division, the shameful history, must end quickly so that our wounds can heal and the monuments of tragedy can be removed. The day the world sees, the pain and longing of those long years, our beautiful secret blossoming, closed their eyes quietly and gathered their hearts. 'Oh, God, have mercy on humanity, on us.' "World Peace Youth Arirang Cultural Center." Ji-ae looked up at the long signboard adorned with colorful hibiscus flowers on both sides. Her heart tingled. Park Jae-hoon's, where could he be buried? Is it painful? "I don't even know if your grandfather is buried here." Ji-ae repeated the story her grand-son had heard many times, as if savoring it once again.

If only he had been the cornerstone of the youth center build-ing, at some point. In the distant past, in a country like the 38th Parallel Demilitarized Zone, which seemed fearful and ominous when he was buried, now, in this place where the atmosphere of fear, like the ashen stones that once gripped the whole body, has disap-peared and the waves of reconciliation are rising. His body must have turned to earth. Isn't wonder the greatest share of humanity, have I existed to be amazed? Where did I read that? A personal life not related to history is worthless... In that sense, both Park Jae-hoon's and Jinhyun's lived valuable lives, reflecting on their own lives. Have I kept the promise to myself? Have I done my best for it? She wanted to believe. For the people with limited space, for those who bring problems to her, for her fellow beings with diverse faces, she worked with obligation and responsibility, with love and joy. Ji-ae measured the sky at the midpoint where the north and south merge, breathed deeply, and expanded her chest.

The Turtle That Never
Loses Its Dream

As Ji-han led the way into the open square, I observed his silhouette from behind and a whimsical thought crossed my mind—wasn't it a poet who once said that departing figures are beautiful? If only our retreating nights of history could be just as lovely... His broad shoulders and straight posture, confidently striding and subtly shaking the ground with each step, filled me with contentment. Indeed, his path forward is not a thorny trail nor a wilderness but a broad avenue stretched out before him. Even if obstacles arise, he will advance bravely forward. Turning to ensure his grandmother was still following, his smile flashed—a smile that catapulted me back in time, igniting emotions reminiscent of my own youthful beauty. In his face, a perfect blend of East and West, I always find comfort. For a fleeting moment, I see Hyun's face in his. Behind the youthful laughter of my grandson, it seems, hides the answer to the human history I've dreamed of and pursued throughout the years.

Then I remembered the oak tree in the backyard of my hometown house, standing resiliently against the storms. In a year when the storms were particularly fierce, when the rain and wind never seemed to cease, I recalled the mystical oak tree of our land, even greener and more mysterious when the sun came out. Long ago, Hyun's voice, which quietly echoed on the shores of New York, whispered to me. "History is a stage where powerful rulers and strong jesters dance. True history is the trace of suffering souls that is unwritten and unheard. Let that river carry us forward. They are not alone. They take us everywhere. Our reunification will be like that. We will definitely achieve it. The Turtle That Never Loses Its Dream will eventually plant its flag at the finish line." Humans should live loving each other in freedom, equality, and peace. Such an era will dawn on this earth. She wanted to believe in that. Just then, a gust of wind swept through the edge of her muffler. She adjusted her muffler and thought of the wind, the wind that shakes the leaves, ripens the grains in the autumn fields, and drops the ripe fruit to the ground, enveloped in the mystery of The Face of the Wind, embracing all humans at both ends of the earth, like a beautiful conclusion akin to home. Ji-han, who now works as a researcher at the United Nations International Institute for Human Rights Issues, also personally assists the research institute for the rights of indigenous peoples where his parents are involved.

Ah, Hyun! The dreams he couldn't fulfill will live on with even greater strength in the depths of others' existence. We should raise a toast of reverence to all of that, and be grateful, because they were possible because they had life, life is a blessing... Ji-ae looked at the white clouds floating in the sky above the lush trees of the DMZ. It was a moment when she felt that this unity of nature and human spirit was the best path that humans could take.

View of the Bound Land
from the Airplane

The next day, Ji-ae boarded a flight to Africa via China. Ji-han would stay in Beijing for a few days before returning to New York. Mi-young had set up a hospital in Bukoba, Tanzania, several years ago to care for women and children wounded by war. She had abruptly left for Chicago when Hyun's KAL plane crashed, only to return and resume her friendship with Ji-ae, working together with her and Jia. Mi-young's letters overflowed with the vibrant vitality of Africa, mixing the red soil and wildlife with the elements of human suffering and wounds. Ji-ae was captivated by her letters, brimming with attachment to life. She unfolded a Korean newspaper she had brought from the airport counter, where they had once sat together at the window seat. There was still some time before the flight departure. A large headline on the society page caught her attention: "Speech by Human Rights Activist Kim Dong-seok."

We are not Koreans living in Korea; we are Korean Americans who love our homeland. As Korean Americans, we should work with the conviction to conquer the Washington Capitol for our homeland without hesitation. That is our patriotic duty. Congressman Kim is passionately delivering his speech. "Youth of our homeland, hold high aspirations in life. Your dreams will surely come true. Do not be discouraged by any circumstances; run with hope. Both of them have been invited by the homeland and are touring the country, delivering strong messages to the general public and youth. Along with them, the dignified and cheerful face of Ryan Kim came to mind. "I am dreaming. The day when young Koreans like us contribute to this society, receive fair treatment, and stand tall at the center of this society, right in the heart of Washington Capitol."

The young man who had come to bid farewell before she left for Korea, the bold young man dreaming of the resonance and success of Koreans in America, Ryan Kim. One day, his photo would be prominently featured in newspapers. Memories resurfaced. Now in his middle age, he managed a successful business and had established a scholarship foundation for second-generation Koreans, confidently nurturing young people who followed in his footsteps. Eventually, the airplane took off. Ji-ae handed the newspaper she had been reading to Ji-han and closed her eyes, instinctively gazing out the window. There, a white cloud drifted by. Ah, at that moment, the barbed wire running across the East Sea and the West Sea! The divided land of the Korean Peninsula, bound by thick chains, came into view! It was a fleeting moment. Ji-ae suddenly held her breath. Her chest ached as if it would tear apart. Was that her homeland, my homeland! The homeland, bound for so long by thick chains. A solitary beetle gnawed at the delicate flesh of her homeland's beauty! But it soon vanished. Was it a dream? Was what she saw a dream, an illusion? In the blink of an eye, the airplane crumpled it into oblivion. Tears streamed down her face, unknowingly. To Ji-ae, her homeland was no longer just a piece of land. It wasn't just a symbol. It was herself. It was the living, breathing herself. Each person living and breathing on the Korean Peninsula was a member of the nation, a brother or sister.

The pain-ridden, writhing flesh of the entire nation! She had clearly seen the division of her homeland, which had previously only existed within the confines of her mind. Her heart tightened, and pain reverberated throughout her body. The thorn pricked and continued to prick for a long time. It was undoubtedly real. She saw it clearly. Calming her pounding heart, she closed her eyes. She recalled the dreadful specter of London Bridge ten years ago, where poor commoners and resistors were imprisoned and starved to death. She had thought then. Is that the true power of history? The countless nameless people who lived behind the scenes of history, spinning the wheels of suffering and leading humanity to prosperity and happiness. "I wept from the observatory while looking at my homeland. Families torn apart, mothers gazing at the southern sky..." The confession left by Park Jae-hoon's on the riverbank of Han, reminiscent of a page in history. And the apparition of the butterfly that hovered over his grave............. Ji-ae placed that butterfly on the three-eight line barbed wire. Unknowingly.

Sound of the Wind

The airplane continued its endless journey forward. Ji-ae leaned back in her seat, closing her eyes in an uncomfortable position. "Only truth, only honesty... Do you know the effect of a small butterfly?" Somewhere, a sound like the flow of a mountain stream echoed softly. Piercing through the metallic sound of the airplane cutting through the air, like milky mist rising white from a place where no one had ever breathed, the sound persisted. "When is the moment a bird truly enjoys freedom and happiness? When it soars high in the sky, believing that is the strongest it can ever be. Even if its wings tear, that pain can turn into happiness. That pain makes it free, and human suffering, after swinging fists at God, inevitably surrenders, singing praises to freedom in glory."

That's when he becomes liberated from everything. The problem lies in the abundance of thorns between people. It's about surreptitiously passing on the thorn bush one received as their lot to others. Both the rich and the poor suffer for this reason. The rich are tormented by the weight of wealth, and the poor suffer from the vast emptiness that swallows them whole. Everyone struggles with hunger and thirst for this reason. It's because of the existence of others. The same goes for countries and nations. However, Ji-ae, the rugged mountain ranges and depths of the earth can become plains due to the collective suffering of a single nation. Dandelions sow seeds with faith. The dandelions of the Korean Peninsula are sowing seeds of peace. From the Azalea Hill of 5,000 years of history to the present... Ah, then... does the question that has tormented her for so long finally unravel? No. Why must our country suffer unjustly for 100 years? The land of miracles, inventing the water clock, celestial globe, observatory, printing, and the world's most scientific script, Hangul, for the first time in the world. A country that has preserved peace for 5,000 years without ever invading another country. The small and proud country, whose imperial house and culture of Japan originated from, has been cruelly plundered and suffered for 36 years, torn apart and groaning with recoil until now. What could be the reason for this?

In that moment, Ji-ae felt the unjustified anger swelling up on her face like an animal, along with the humiliation, injustice, and rage. Time passed. Eventually, the humiliation, anger, and injustice strangely disappeared. The dark and tangled threads melted away and vanished. Standing in the dark cave where beasts wriggled as if about to burst into tears, she was suddenly dazzled by the clear morning sky and sunrise. Every cell in her body seemed to wriggle with joy, as if dancing happily. "Truth, it's all about truth. Only honesty, returning to the basics of humanity." That voice was like the wind, the voice that had traveled around the entire Earth and back. It sounded like the voice that had traveled through layers of fallen leaves piled high with time, beyond countless starry realms, in an instant, no, from eternity to eternity. Ji-ae became a point in the universe. She immersed herself in that sound. It was a new song, an invitation to everyone on Earth. The scent of a steel flower brushed her nose. Whirr, whirr, flutter, like a bird, a butterfly flew. She joined them, soaring with iridescent colors!

After returning from Africa, several days passed for Ji-ae.

Having slept deeply through the long night, Ji-ae dreamed at dawn. In her dream, she was standing at the 'Peace Outlook' in Ganghwa Island.

Located at latitude 37.75, the fourth-largest island in Korea, situated between North and South Korea, she held Park Jae-hoon's urn in her hand. She opened it and began to scatter its contents, raising her arms.

At that moment, the wind blew. A wind as large as the wings of a giant dove descended from the sky. Following that wind, a red sun rose from the east. A blazing ball of light, circling and burning, rose as if spreading the wings that a giant eagle had seized. In the center of that light, a round and massive sun... swirling brilliance as if embracing the mountains and swirling round and round, she scattered the remaining ashes as if offering them to the burning sun.

Fly, fly,
Eagle, fly
Fly like an eagle
Plant equality and truth in the hearts of humanity
Eradicate poverty, misery, hatred, and war
Let the world overflow with peace

Oh, peace
Be love
Only truth, only truth shall blossom
Forever blossom, blossom
Only truth, only love, only peace, only peace...!

From the wings of the eagle, tens of thousands, millions of butterflies soared like drawing seven rainbows
Raindrops fell like dew. It was dazzling! Riding rainbows, people from all over the world rose together. Laughing like blooming flowers, fluttering seven-colored petals, flying and flying...
The world danced in one light, in the light!

The peace of the world and love.

Arirang Korean Folk Song

Arirang, Arirang, Arariyo
Arirang gogaero neomeoganda
Nareul beorigo gashineun nimeun
Simnido motgaseo balbyeongnanda

Arirang, Arirang, Arariyo
Going up hills and Mt. Arariyo
If you forsake me to go Arariyo

ARIRANG
ARIRANG
ARARIYO